SHEET PAN COOKBOOK

Easy and Delicious One-Pan Recipes
for Everyday Family Cooking

CHRISTOPHER LESTER

Contents

WELCOME

Welcome to the world of sheet pan cooking. As a passionate home cook and cookbook author, I am excited to share the magic of one-pan cooking with you. My journey into the world of food began in my grandmother's cozy kitchen, where the aromas of her homemade dishes filled the air and brought our family together. These cherished memories instilled in me a deep love of cooking and a desire to create dishes that not only nourish the body but also warm the heart.

I have tried many cooking methods over the years, but the pan has become my true favorite. Its simplicity and versatility are unrivaled, making it perfect for today's busy families. With a single pan, you can make a variety of delicious and healthy dishes that require minimal cleanup – something every home cook can appreciate. The ease and convenience of sheet pan cooking can truly be a game-changer in your kitchen.

What I love most about the sheet pan is its ability to bring people together. Whether it's a hectic weekday dinner or a relaxed Sunday brunch, these recipes are designed to be shared and enjoyed by loved ones. The convenience of one-pan cooking allows for more time at the table with family and friends, creating an unforgettable experience. The joy of shared meals and the creation of these lasting memories are what truly make sheet pan cooking special.

In this cookbook, I've compiled a collection of my favorite sheet pan recipes, which are easy to prepare and incredibly delicious. From hearty breakfasts and colorful vegetable side dishes to succulent meats and delectable desserts, there's something for everyone.

I invite you to join me on this culinary journey and explore the pleasures of pan-cooking. Let's make every meal an opportunity to connect, savor, and celebrate the simple joys of life. Happy cooking!

MASTERING THE ESSENTIALS OF SHEET PAN COOKING

Pan cooking has revolutionized my approach to home cooking, offering the perfect blend of simplicity and sophistication. As someone who grew up surrounded by the cozy aromas of my grandmother's kitchen, I've always been passionate about creating dishes that bring people together. Over the years, I've tried many cooking techniques, but sheet pan cooking remains my favorite.

There are several reasons why sheet pan cooking is a staple in my kitchen and why I believe it should be in yours as well:

- **Simplicity:** Minimal prep makes pan cooking a breeze, especially on busy weekdays.
- **Versatility:** From breakfast to dinner and even dessert, the pan-cooking possibilities are endless.
- **Efficiency:** Cooking in just one pan saves time, allowing you to enjoy your food.
- **Healthy cooking:** Fresh, wholesome ingredients are often the protagonists of roasting recipes, allowing you to eat healthily without sacrificing flavor.

NECESSARY TOOLS AND EQUIPMENT

In order to start cooking, you need to have a few basic tools:

- **Sheet pans:** Choose sturdy pans that can withstand high heat and allow for even cooking. My favorite option is a standard half-sheet pan.
- **Parchment paper or silicone mats:** These are lifesavers that prevent sticking and make cleanup easier.
- **Cutting board and knives:** Essential for efficient preparation of ingredients.
- **Mixing bowls:** Ideal for mixing ingredients with seasonings before placing them on the baking tray.
- **Tongs and spatulas:** Handy for flipping and serving your delicious creations.

TYPES OF SHEET PANS

Understanding the different types of pans will help you choose the right one for your needs:

- **Standard half-sheet pan:** The most common size, approximately 18x13 inches, is perfect for most recipes.
- **Quarter sheet pan:** Smaller and perfect for side dishes or small portions.
- **Jelly Roll Mold:** Slightly smaller than a half-sheet pan, with high sides, great for baking and frying.

CLEANING AND CARE OF SHEET PANS

Proper care and maintenance of your skillet extends its life and improves its performance. Here are some tips based on my personal experience:

- **Direct cleaning:** Wash your skillet with warm, soapy water after each use. Don't leave food residue for long periods. I always make it a rule to clean immediately after dinner.
- **Don't use abrasive cleaners:** Use a soft sponge or cloth to avoid scratching the surface. For burnt stains, a mixture of baking soda and water works great.
- **Wipe thoroughly:** To prevent rust, be sure to dry the pans completely. My grandmother always taught me to wipe them down with a kitchen towel immediately after washing them.
- **Regular deep cleaning:** Periodically soak your pans in hot water with dish soap and then gently scrub them to remove any accumulated dirt. This way, they will look and perform like new.
- **Storage:** Store your pans in a dry place, stacking them neatly to avoid scratches and dents. I like to keep them on hand since I use them so often.

PERFECTING YOUR SHEET PAN MEALS

To get the most out of your sheet pan meals, it is important to master the art of preparing ingredients. The key is to cook all ingredients evenly. Here are a few tips to help you always achieve perfectly cooked dishes:

- **Cut evenly:** Cut vegetables and proteins into equal-sized pieces. This ensures that everything cooks at the same speed, preventing some ingredients from overcooking and others from undercooking.
- **Layers:** Place denser vegetables like potatoes and carrots in the pan first, as they require longer cooking times. Lighter vegetables, such as bell peppers and zucchini, can be added later in the cooking process.
- **Spacing:** Avoid overcrowding the pan. Give ingredients enough room to roast and caramelize, not steam. This will diversify the flavor and texture of your dish.
- **Time:** Add ingredients in stages, focusing on their cooking time. For example, add quick-cooking shrimp or tender greens at the end to avoid overcooking.

BALANCE FLAVORS AND TEXTURES

A great sheet pan dish is not only about even cooking but also about a harmonious balance of flavors and textures:

- **Flavor Profiles:** Use a combination of fresh herbs, fragrant spices, and marinades to enhance the flavors of ingredients. Some fragrant herbs or a squeeze of lemon juice can add brightness and depth to a dish.
- **Contrast textures:** Combine ingredients with different textures. Combining crunchy roasted vegetables with tender proteins and creamy sauces can create a delightful dish experience.
- **Layers of seasoning:** Season ingredients at different stages of cooking. Start with a basic seasoning before roasting and finish with salt, pepper, or dressing just before serving.

NUTRITIONAL BENEFITS

Cooking on a sheet pan is not only convenient, but it's also a great way to prepare healthy and nutritious meals:

- **Whole Foods:** Sheet pan recipes often utilize fresh vegetables, whole grains, and lean proteins for a complete nutritious meal.
- **Healthy Fats:** roasting in a small amount of olive oil or avocado oil enhances flavor while providing heart-healthy fats.
- **Reduced sodium:** By cooking at home, you can control the amount of salt you use, reducing your sodium intake compared to processed or restaurant food.

SUBSTITUTING INGREDIENTS FOR HEALTHIER OPTIONS

Small substitutions can significantly increase the nutritional value of your sheet pan-cooked meals:

- **Vegetables:** Replace starchy vegetables like potatoes with lower-carb options like cauliflower or turnips. Use a variety of colorful vegetables to provide a mix of nutrients.
- **Protein:** Favor lean proteins such as chicken breast and turkey or plant-based foods like tofu or tempeh. If you use red meat, choose lean cuts.
- **Grains:** Replace ordinary grains with whole grains such as quinoa, farro, or brown rice. They have more fiber and nutrients.
- **Fats:** Use healthy natural fats (olive oil, coconut oil/ avocado oil) instead of butter or other saturated fats. These healthy fats enhance the flavor of your meals while providing essential fatty acids to your body.
- **Sweeteners:** If your recipe calls for sweetness, use natural sweeteners (honey or maple syrup) in moderation instead of refined sugars.

MY PERSONAL TIPS

- **Prepare ahead of time:** One of my favorite tricks is to prep ingredients the night before. It makes it easier to assemble and prepare dinner the next day.
- **Family Favorite Meals:** My kids love to help with pan cooking, especially if it involves arranging vegetables or adding their favorite toppings. It's a fun way to get them involved in the kitchen.
- **Experiment with flavors:** Don't be afraid to mix and match different herbs, spices, and marinades. Some of my best recipes have come from experimenting with what I had on hand.

By following these basic principles and caring for your equipment, you will master the art of pan cooking. It's not just a method - it's a way to bring case, joy, and flavor to your everyday family meals.

SEASONAL MAGIC

The sheet pan is incredibly versatile, making it the perfect method for using seasonal ingredients and creating festive dishes for holidays and special occasions. By adapting recipes to the freshest produce each season has to offer, you can improve the flavor and nutritional value of your dishes.

Spring is a time of renewal with fresh, vibrant vegetables. Think tender greens, crisp radishes, and sweet peas.

During the summer season of abundance, fruits and vegetables are at the peak of ripeness.

Fall brings with it hearty, comforting foods that are perfect for warming dishes.

Winter's chill calls for robust, nutrient-rich vegetables and warming spices.

IDEAS FOR HOLIDAYS AND SPECIAL OCCASIONS

Sheet pan meals are also perfect for holidays and special occasions, allowing you to create impressive dishes with minimal stress.

THANKSGIVING

Turkey breast and side dish: Bake turkey breast along with Brussels sprouts, sweet potatoes, and cranberries. This simplified version of a traditional Thanksgiving meal saves time and effort.

Stuffed Mushrooms: Fill large mushroom caps with savory stuffing and roast until golden and soft.

CHRISTMAS

Beef Tenderloin with Herb Crust: Roast beef tenderloin in a crust of fresh herbs, garlic, and olive oil. Add an assortment of winter vegetables like potatoes, carrots, and parsnips for a festive dish.

Festive Baked Vegetables: Prepare a colorful assortment of baked vegetables, including red and green bell peppers, zucchini, and cherry tomatoes, to create a visually appealing side dish.

PASSOVER

Ham in Honey Glaze: Roast a spiral-sliced ham in a honey-mustard glaze. Surround it with spring vegetables such as asparagus and carrots.

Salmon with Lemon Dill: For an easy and elegant Easter dish, serve salmon fillets with lemon slices, fresh dill, and new potatoes.

FOURTH OF JULY

BBQ Chicken with Corn: Roast chicken thighs in a tangy BBQ sauce; add corn on the cob and bell peppers. This simple and versatile dish pairs well for summer festivities.

Berry Cobbler: Use fresh summer berries to make a simple cobbler. Roast them with a sprinkle of crumble to make a patriotic dessert.

BIRTHDAY CELEBRATION

Pizza Night: Prepare pizza on a sheet with your favorite toppings. Have everyone make their own portion of pizza to their liking for a fun, interactive meal.

Chocolate Lava Cake: Bake individual chocolate cakes with a gooey center and serve them with fresh berries and whipped cream.

By adapting recipes for sheet pans, adding seasonal ingredients, and developing dishes for special occasions, you can turn every meal into a celebration. Take advantage of the bounty of each season and the joy of holiday cooking to create dishes that will satisfy both the palate and the senses.

Breakfast & Brunch

Frittata with Broccoli and Cheese	16
Pancake with Strawberries	18
Homemade Granola	20
Avocado Boats with Bacon	22
French Toast	24

FRITTATA WITH BROCCOLI AND CHEESE

The frittata is an Italian dish that originated centuries ago and is often considered the Italian version of an omelet. Unlike an omelet, which is cooked and rolled on the stovetop, a frittata is usually started on the stovetop and finished in the oven, or in this case, baked completely in the oven on a sheet pan for ease and convenience.

When I was a kid, my grandmother made a similar frittata using whatever vegetables and leftovers were in the fridge. It was a versatile dish that could be served for any meal of the day, and it always seemed like a special treat. She often served it with a simple salad and a crust of bread.

VARIATIONS:

Vegetables: *bell peppers, spinach, mushrooms.* **Proteins:** *cooked chicken, bacon, sausage.* **Cheese:** *feta, goat cheese, gruyere.*

8 servings   15 minutes   25 minutes

INGREDIENTS:

- 2 cups broccoli florets, chopped
- 1 cup peas
- 1 yellow onion (70 g), finely chopped
- 1 cup cheddar (or cheese of your choice), shredded
- 12 large eggs

- ½ cup (120 ml) milk (whole or 2%)
- 2 cloves garlic, minced
- Salt and pepper, to taste
- Fresh thyme or parsley, for garnish
- Olive oil, for greasing

HOW TO COOK:

1. Preheat the oven to 375°F (190°C). Grease a rimmed baking sheet (about 18x13 inches) with oil or line it with parchment paper.
2. Heat a bit of olive oil in a skillet over medium heat. Fry the chopped onion and garlic for 5 minutes until they are translucent.
3. Add the broccoli florets to the skillet and cook for another 2-3 minutes until they are completely tender. Remove from heat and set aside.
4. In a bowl, whisk eggs, whole milk, salt, and pepper until smooth. Add shredded cheddar cheese.
5. Spread the sautéed vegetables and peas evenly on the prepared baking sheet.
6. Pour the egg cheese mixture over the vegetables, making sure it evenly coats them. Using a spatula, gently stir the ingredients so that the vegetables and cheese are well distributed.
7. Place the frittata in the oven and bake for 20-25 minutes until the eggs are set and the top is lightly golden.
8. Let it cool for a few minutes.
9. Cut the frittata into squares and garnish with fresh thyme or parsley before serving.

NUTRITIONAL INFO (PER SERVING):

Calories: 200, Carbohydrates: 4 g, Cholesterol: 265 mg, Sodium: 280 mg, Protein: 14 g, Fats: 14 g, Saturated Fat: 6 g, Sugar: 2 g, Fiber: 1 g

PANCAKE WITH STRAWBERRIES

One of the best things about sheet pan pancakes is that they fit easily into your morning routine. You can mix the dry ingredients the night before, and in the morning, all you have to do is combine them with the wet ingredients and bake.

If you're hosting a brunch or have a large family, sheet pan pancakes are a lifesaver. They eliminate the need to stand over the griddle, flipping individual pancakes, allowing you to give more time to your guests. In many families, pancake breakfasts are a cherished tradition. Kids love to help with this recipe, especially when it comes to adding the toppings. Let them arrange the fruit and chocolate chips themselves – it's a fun, creative activity that will also keep them engrossed in their breakfast.

VARIATIONS:

This recipe is incredibly versatile. You can change up the filling depending on what you have on hand or what's in season. Try adding blueberries, raspberries, bananas, or even peanut butter. For an extra nutritional boost, add ½ cup of rolled oats and some flaxseed or chia seeds.

12 servings   15 minutes   25 minutes

INGREDIENTS:

- 2 cups (260 g) all-purpose flour/ whole-grain flour/gluten-free flour
- 2 Tbsp. white sugar
- 1 Tbsp. baking powder
- ½ tsp. baking soda
- ½ tsp. salt
- 2 large eggs

- 2 cups (480 ml) buttermilk/almond milk + 1 tablespoon of lemon juice
- ¼ cup (60 ml) unsalted butter, melted and cooled
- 1 tsp. vanilla extract
- 1 cup (170 g) fresh strawberries, sliced
- ½ cup (170 g) chocolate chips

HOW TO COOK:

1. Preheat the oven to 425°F (220°C). Grease a large baking sheet (about 13x18 inches) with cooking spray/oil, or line it with parchment paper.
2. Combine flour, sugar, salt, baking soda, and baking powder in a bowl.
3. In a separate bowl, mix buttermilk, eggs, melted butter, and vanilla extract until smooth.
4. Gently mix the wet and dry ingredients in a bowl until just combined. Be careful not to over-mix; it's okay if a few lumps remain.
5. Spread the pancake batter on the greased baking sheet. Make sure to spread it evenly across the pan to ensure even cooking. If the batter is too thick in some areas, it may not bake properly.
6. Spread the sliced strawberries and chocolate chips evenly over the top of the batter.
7. Place the pancake in the preheated oven and bake for 15-20 minutes until the top is golden. Check it with a toothpick in the center.
8. Allow the pancake to cool for a few minutes. Cut into squares and serve warm with a topping of your choice (maple syrup, whipped cream, or extra fresh fruit).
9. Store the leftovers in the fridge and easily reheat in the oven or microwave. They also freeze well – just separate the layers with parchment paper and store them in a Ziplock bag.

NUTRITIONAL INFO (PER SERVING):

Calories: 210, Carbohydrates: 28 g, Cholesterol: 45 mg, Sodium: 220 mg, Protein: 4 g, Fats: 9 g, Sugar: 9 g, Fiber: 1 g

HOMEMADE GRANOLA

Granola has always been a favorite dish in our family. I remember the first time I made it: the tantalizing aroma of toasted oats and nuts filled the kitchen, instantly drawing everyone in. My kids love to help, especially when it comes to mixing and adding their favorite ingredients.

One summer, we decided to make granola bars for traveling. Using this basic recipe, we added some peanut butter and a few chocolate chips. The bars were a hit, and it turned into a fun tradition to modify the recipe for different occasions.

VARIATIONS:

Feel free to diversify your granola by adding your favorite nuts, seeds, and dried fruits. Coconut flakes, pumpkin seeds, and dried apricots are great additions.

8 servings   10 minutes   30 minutes

INGREDIENTS:

- 3 cups (240 g) old-fashioned rolled oats
- 1 cup (150 g) mixed nuts (almonds, walnuts, pecans), roughly chopped
- ½ cup (70 g) sunflower seeds
- ½ cup (60 g) dried cranberries
- ½ cup (75 g) dried raisins
- ¼ cup (35 g) flax seeds
- ¼ cup (35 g) chia seeds
- 1/3 cup (80 ml) honey/maple syrup/ agave syrup/brown rice syrup
- ¼ cup (60 ml) coconut oil, melted
- 1 tsp. vanilla extract
- 1 tsp. ground cinnamon
- ½ tsp. salt

HOW TO COOK:

1. Preheat the oven to 325°F (165°C). Line a sheet pan with parchment paper.
2. Mix the rolled oats, nuts, sunflower seeds, flax seeds, chia seeds, ground cinnamon, and salt in a bowl. Mix well.
3. Combine honey/maple syrup, melted coconut oil, and vanilla extract in another bowl until fully combined.
4. Stir the wet and dry ingredients until everything is evenly coated.
5. Spread the grain mixture evenly on the lined baking sheet. Press it down lightly with the back of a spoon or spatula.
6. Bake the oat granola for 25-30 minutes until golden and fragrant. Stir every 10 minutes.
7. If you prefer a lumpier granola, press the mixture down firmly before baking, and don't stir it halfway through.
8. Allow it to cool completely. Once cooled, add dried cranberries and raisins.
9. Store the granola with additives in a jar at room temperature for up to two weeks.

NUTRITIONAL INFO (PER SERVING):

Calories: 320, Carbohydrates: 42 g, Cholesterol: 40 mg, Sodium: 90 mg, Protein: 7 g, Fats: 15 g, Sugar: 18 g, Fiber: 5 g

AVOCADO BOATS WITH BACON

I first came across this recipe during a family brunch where I wanted to serve something healthy yet non-boring. My cousin, who follows a strict keto diet, was thrilled to see a dish that met her dietary needs but still tasted amazing. The creamy texture of the baked avocado combined with the savory eggs and crispy bacon create a hearty dish. We experimented with different toppings and found that the hot sauce gave the dish the perfect spiciness.

Using a sheet pan makes cleanup a breeze, and you can easily make several servings at once, making this dish perfect for brunch or family meals.

VARIATIONS:

For a change, try adding shredded cheese on top before baking to give the dish a cheesy touch. Another tasty option is to sprinkle smoked paprika or chili flakes for extra flavor.

4 servings   10 minutes   20 minutes

INGREDIENTS:

- 2 large ripe avocados, cut in half lengthwise
- 4 large eggs
- 4 strips of bacon (60 g)
- Salt and pepper to taste
- ¼ cup (30 g) chives/green onions, chopped
- hot sauce or salsa, for serving (optional)

HOW TO COOK:

1. Set the oven to 425°F (220°C). Line a sheet pan with parchment paper or aluminum foil.
2. Place the raw bacon strips on a sheet pan and cook for 10-12 minutes until crispy.
3. Transfer the crispy bacon strips to a paper towel-lined plate to drain and cool. Then, cut the bacon into small pieces.
4. Leave the fat from the bacon on the baking pan for extra flavor.
5. Scoop out about 1-2 tablespoons of avocado pulp from the center of each half to make room for the eggs. (Tip: save the avocado pulp for another use, such as guacamole or smoothies).
6. Place the avocado halves on the same baking tray as the bacon grease so they are stable and won't tip over (you can use crumpled foil to make nests for stability).
7. Crack an egg into each avocado half. Season with salt and pepper.
8. Place the sheet pan in the oven and cook the boats for 15-20 minutes until the eggs are set.
9. Once baked, sprinkle the avocado boats with crumbled bacon and chopped chives. If desired, top with hot sauce or salsa.
10. Enjoy baked avocado boats warm.

NUTRITIONAL INFO (PER SERVING):

Calories: 250, Carbohydrates: 8 g, Cholesterol: 210 mg, Sodium: 350 mg, Protein: 9 g, Fats: 20 g, Sugar: 1 g, Fiber: 7 g

FRENCH TOAST

This recipe for sheet pan French toast has become a weekend favorite in my family. On Sunday mornings, my kids and I would gather in the kitchen, whip up the custard, and spread the bread. The aroma of vanilla and cinnamon filling the house is a cherished memory that brings a smile to my face every time. This is the perfect recipe for family gatherings or brunch with friends.

This French toast can be made the night before. Just place it on a sheet pan, cover it with plastic wrap, and put it away in the refrigerator. In the morning, just bake it and enjoy!

VARIATIONS:

Brioche and challah are my top choices for this recipe because of their rich texture and ability to absorb custard. However, you can experiment with other types of bread, such as sourdough or whole wheat.

6 servings   15 minutes   25 minutes

INGREDIENTS:

- 8 large eggs
- 1 cup (240 ml) whole milk
- ¼ cup (50 g) granulated sugar
- 1 cup (240 ml) heavy cream
- 1 tsp. vanilla extract
- ½ tsp. ground cinnamon
- ¼ tsp. ground nutmeg
- Pinch of salt
- 12 slices of bread (brioche/challah), thick cut
- 2 tbsp. unsalted butter, melted

FOR THE STUFFING:
- 2 bananas, sliced
- 1 cup (150 g) mixed berries (raspberries, blueberries, etc.)
- ¼ cup (60 ml) maple syrup
- ¼ cup (30 g) chopped nuts (almonds, pecans)
- Powdered sugar for dusting (optional)
- Fresh mint leaves for garnish (optional)

1. Preheat the oven to 375°F (190°C). Grease a large baking pan (18x13 inches/ 45x33 cm) with nonstick spray or butter.
2. Mix eggs, milk, cream, sugar, vanilla extract, cinnamon, nutmeg, and salt in a bowl.
3. Place the bread slices in a single layer on the prepared sheet pan, overlapping slightly if necessary.
4. Pour the egg-milk custard over the bread so that all the slices are well coated. Leave for 5-10 minutes to allow the bread to soak up the custard.
5. Pour the melted butter over the top of the bread.
6. Bake for 20-25 minutes until golden brown and puffy.
7. Allow to cool for a few minutes.
8. Top with your favorite fruits and nuts, and sprinkle with powdered sugar as you desire, adding your personal touch to the dish.
9. Drizzle the fluffy French toast with maple syrup and garnish with fresh mint leaves.
10. Serve warm and enjoy!

NUTRITIONAL INFO (PER SERVING):

Calories: 450, Carbohydrates: 52 g, Cholesterol: 210 mg, Sodium: 340 mg, Protein: 12 g, Fats: 22 g, Sugar: 20 g, Fiber: 4 g

Appetizers & Snacks

Cheese Garlic Breadsticks	28
Pizza alla Bismark	30
Stuffed Peppers	32
Cauliflower and Broccoli Bites	34
Sheet Pan Nachos	36

CHEESE GARLIC BREADSTICKS

American adaptations of Italian grissini breadsticks have resulted in a softer version that pairs well with a variety of Italian American dishes. Grissini were baked in Italy's Piedmont region back in the 17th century and are rumored to have been created to ease the digestion of a young duke. Traditionally, these breadsticks were thin and crispy, often flavored with rosemary or other herbs. The addition of cheese and garlic gives them a rich and savory flavor, making them a favorite in pizzerias and home kitchens alike. The baking method on a baking sheet simplifies the cooking process, ensuring even baking and easy serving.

VARIATIONS:

For a stronger garlic flavor, opt for roasted garlic instead of raw. For a unique flavor, experiment with different cheeses, such as cheddar, Gouda, or a blend of Italian cheeses. To flavor the melted butter, add fresh herbs like rosemary or thyme.

12 servings   15 minutes   20 minutes

INGREDIENTS:

- 1 cup (240 ml) warm water (110°F/43°C)
- 2¼ tsp. active dry yeast (1 packet)
- 1 tbsp granulated sugar
- 2½ cups (300 g) all-purpose flour
- 1 tsp. salt
- 2 Tbsp. (30 ml) olive oil (plus extra for greasing)
- 3 cloves garlic, minced

- 3 Tbsp. (45 g) unsalted butter, melted
- 1½ cups (170 g) shredded mozzarella cheese
- ½ cup (50 g) grated Parmesan cheese
- 1 tsp. dried oregano (optional)
- 1 tsp. dried parsley (optional)

HOW TO COOK:

1. Combine the warm water, granulated sugar, and a packet of yeast in a bowl. Stir and let stand for 5-10 minutes to allow the yeast to foam.
2. Mix the flour and salt in a bowl. Make a well in the center and add the yeast mixture and olive oil. Stir until the dough forms.
3. Sprinkle flour over the surface and knead the dough until smooth.
4. Put the dough in a greased bowl. Cover the bowl with the dough with a damp towel and leave for 1 hour until it has doubled in size.
5. Preheat the oven to 375°F (190°C). Grease the sheet pan with olive oil.
6. Knead the dough and transfer it to the sheet pan.
7. Mix the melted butter and minced garlic. Brush onto the dough. Sprinkle mozzarella and grated parmesan on top. Top with dried oregano and parsley if desired.
8. Bake for 15 minutes until golden and cheese is bubbling and lightly browned.
9. Let the breadsticks cool slightly, and then cut them into strips. Serve warm.

NUTRITIONAL INFO (PER SERVING):

Calories: 180, Carbohydrates: 22 g, Cholesterol: 15 mg, Sodium: 240 mg, Protein: 6 g, Fats: 22 g, Sugar: 1 g, Fiber: 1 g

PIZZA ALLA BISMARK

Pizza alla Bismark is named after the first Chancellor of the German Empire. Bismark was known for his love of hearty dishes, often including eggs. It is said that he could eat a dozen eggs in one sitting. Despite its German name, Pizza alla Bismark has strong roots in Italian cuisine.

The creamy egg yolk complements the savory flavor of the prosciutto or ham, and the spinach adds a fresh, slightly bitter note. Whether you prefer a runny yolk, which gives each slice a rich, sauce-like texture, or a fully cooked egg, which provides a more substantial portion of protein, this pizza will satisfy a variety of tastes.

You can diversify the pizza with different cheeses, additional vegetables, or even a sprinkling of herbs like thyme or rosemary.

VARIATIONS:

Experiment with different cheeses, such as fontina, goat cheese, or pecorino, for a unique flavor profile. For a vegetarian version, omit the prosciutto or ham and add more vegetables like bell peppers, mushrooms, or artichokes. To spice up the dish, add red pepper flakes or drizzle with chili oil before serving.

4-6 servings   20 minutes   15-20 minutes

INGREDIENTS:

PIZZA DOUGH:

- 3½-4 cups (420-480 g) all-purpose flour (plus more for dusting)
- 1 packet (2¼ tsp./7 g) active dry yeast
- 1½ cups (360 ml) warm water (110°F/45°C)
- 2 Tbsp. (30 ml) olive oil
- 2 tsp. (10 g) sugar
- 2 tsp. (10 g) salt

TOPPINGS:

- 1 cup (240 ml) tomato sauce
- 2 cups (200 g) shredded mozzarella
- ½ cup (50 g) grated Parmesan cheese
- 4-6 slices of prosciutto/ham
- 2 cups (60 g) fresh spinach leaves
- 4 large eggs
- Fresh basil leaves for garnish

HOW TO COOK:

1. Dissolve the sugar in the warm water and add the yeast.
2. Gradually add salt, olive oil, and flour, mixing until you get the dough. Knead for 8-10 minutes until elastic. Put the dough in a warm place for 1-2 hours until it has doubled in size.
3. Preheat the oven to 475°F (245°C).
4. Obeam the risen dough to release air bubbles. Roll the dough out on a floured surface into a rectangle that will fit your sheet pan. Transfer the dough to a lightly oiled sheet pan.
5. Pour the tomato sauce evenly over the dough. Sprinkle with shredded mozzarella and grated parmesan. Place slices of prosciutto/ham on top and arrange fresh spinach leaves on top.
6. Make 4 small indentations in the filling and gently scramble an egg into each.
7. Bake for 10-15 minutes until the eggs are cooked to your liking. Garnish with fresh basil leaves. Slice and serve immediately.

NUTRITIONAL INFO (PER SERVING):

Calories: 350, Carbohydrates: 35 g, Cholesterol: 180 mg, Sodium: 800 mg, Protein: 18 g, Fats: 15 g, Sugar: 3 g, Fiber: 2 g

Appetizers & Snacks

STUFFED PEPPERS

Served as a main course or a hearty appetizer, these stuffed peppers are sure to be a hit at any party. The bright colors and enticing flavor make them as visually appealing as they are delicious.

In Mediterranean cuisine, peppers are often stuffed with a mixture of rice, herbs, and sometimes meat. In this recipe, the combination of cheese and bacon brings together a rich, creamy texture and smoky flavor. Wrapping the peppers in bacon fills each piece with a savory, crispy crust that contrasts beautifully with the tender peppers and creamy filling.

VARIATIONS:

For vegetarians, replace the bacon with sautéed mushrooms, spinach, cooked quinoa, or rice. Add crushed red pepper flakes, chopped sun-dried tomatoes or olives to the filling. This will spice up the dish.

4 servings   20 minutes   25 minutes

INGREDIENTS:

- 4 large bell peppers (red, yellow, orange), halved and de-seeded
- 1 cup (240 g) cottage cheese/ricotta
- 1 cup (120 g) mozzarella, shredded
- ½ cup (50 g) Parmesan/cheddar, grated
- 1 small onion (50 g), finely chopped
- 2 cloves garlic, minced

- 1 tablespoon olive oil
- 1 teaspoon dried oregano
- 1 teaspoon dried basil
- ½ tsp. salt
- ½ tsp. black pepper
- 8 slices bacon/prosciutto
- fresh parsley, for garnish

HOW TO COOK:

1. Preheat the oven to 375°F (190°C).
2. Heat olive oil in a pan over low-medium heat.
3. Add the onion and garlic. Fry until softened, about 3-4 minutes.
4. Combine the fried onion and garlic with cottage cheese, mozzarella cheese, parmesan cheese, oregano, basil, salt, and black pepper. Mix well.
5. Stuff the pepper halves with cottage cheese, filling them generously.
6. Wrap bacon slices around pepper halves. Secure with a toothpick if necessary.
7. Arrange the stuffed pepper halves in a single layer on a sheet pan.
8. Bake for 25 minutes until the bacon is crispy.
9. Sprinkle with fresh parsley. Drizzle the peppers with the hot sauce before serving.

NUTRITIONAL INFO (PER SERVING):

Calories: 320, Carbohydrates: 8 g, Cholesterol: 60 mg, Sodium: 700 mg, Protein: 18 g, Fats: 24 g, Sugar: 4 g, Fiber: 2 g

CAULIFLOWER AND BROCCOLI BITES

Historically, roasted vegetables have been a staple dish in many cultures due to their simplicity and the ease of enhancing natural flavor with just a few ingredients. This recipe is a modern interpretation of these timeless traditions. The combination of cauliflower and broccoli not only makes the dish visually appealing but also brings together textures and flavors that are both hearty and nutritious.

VARIATIONS:

In the last 5 minutes of roasting, add shredded cheddar or mozzarella to give the dish a cheesy flavor. For a spicy flavor, experiment with other spices such as cumin, curry powder, or chili flakes.

6-8 servings   15 minutes   25 minutes

INGREDIENTS:

- 1 medium head cauliflower (1½ lb./700 g), cut into florets
- 1 medium head broccoli (1 lb./450 g), cut into florets
- 3 Tbsp. (45 ml) olive oil
- 1 tsp. garlic powder
- 1 tsp. smoked paprika

- ½ tsp. cayenne pepper
- 1 tsp. salt
- ½ tsp. black pepper
- 1 lemon, zest and juice
- ¼ cup (25 g) Parmesan, grated

HOW TO COOK:

1. Preheat the oven to 425°F (220°C). Line a large sheet pan with parchment paper or lightly grease it.
2. In a large bowl, combine the cauliflower and broccoli florets. Make sure the cauliflower and broccoli florets are cut equally to ensure even cooking.
3. Drizzle the florets with olive oil. Add garlic powder, smoked paprika, cayenne pepper, salt, and black pepper. Mix well so all pieces are evenly coated with oil and spices.
4. Spread the seasoned cauliflower and broccoli evenly on the prepared baking sheet.
5. Bake for 20-25 minutes until the vegetables are tender and lightly browned around the edges. Halfway through the baking time, flip the vegetables to ensure even cooking.
6. Once baked, remove from oven, and immediately sprinkle with lemon zest, lemon juice, and grated cheese, if desired. Stir to mix. Skip the parmesan or substitute with nutritional yeast for a vegan version.
7. Serve hot as a garnish or appetizer.

NUTRITIONAL INFO (PER SERVING):

Calories: 150, Carbohydrates: 10 g, Cholesterol: 0 mg, Sodium: 350 mg, Protein: 4 g, Fats: 11 g, Sugar: 3 g, Fiber: 4 g

SHEET PAN NACHOS

Ignacio Nacho Anaya first made this dish in 1943 for a group of American military spouses in Mexico when they came to his restaurant after closing time. Using what was on hand, Anaya stuffed tortilla chips with melted cheese and pickled jalapenos, giving rise to the iconic appetizer. Nachos are a fantastic example of Tex-Mex cuisine that blends Mexican and American culinary traditions.

In addition to traditional fillings, bold chefs experiment with unique ingredients such as barbecue pork, Buffalo chicken, or even dessert nachos with sweet shavings and chocolate coating. Skillet nachos are incredibly versatile. You can make them to suit a variety of dietary preferences, including vegetarian, vegan, or gluten-free.

VARIATIONS:

Vegetarians can omit the ground beef and add beans or roasted vegetables such as bell peppers and corn. For spicy nachos, add fresh jalapenos or hot sauce before baking. Use cooked shrimp or crab meat to give the dish a seafood twist.

6 servings   15 minutes   10 minutes

INGREDIENTS:

- 1 lb. (450 g) ground beef/shredded rotisserie chicken/diced cooked chicken breast
- 1 packet taco seasoning mix (1 oz./28 g)
- ¼ cup (60 ml) water
- 1 bag tortilla chips (12 oz./340 g)
- 2 cups (200 g) cheddar, shredded
- 1 cup (100 g) Monterey Jack cheese, shredded

- 1 can (15 oz./425 g) black beans, drained and rinsed
- ½ cup (120 ml) pickled jalapeños, sliced
- ½ cup red onion, diced
- 1 cup tomatoes, diced
- ½ cup (120 ml) black olives, sliced
- 1 cup (240 ml) guacamole
- ½ cup (120 ml) sour cream
- ¼ cup fresh cilantro, chopped

HOW TO COOK:

1. Preheat the oven to 400°F (200°C).
2. In a large skillet, fry the ground beef over medium heat until browned. Drain excess fat. Add taco seasoning mix and water. Simmer for 5 minutes until thickened.
3. Place a layer of tortilla chips on a large sheet pan. Spread the seasoned ground beef over the chips. To prevent the chips from getting soggy, place them in a single layer and don't overload them with too much filling.
4. Sprinkle shredded Cheddar and Monterey Jack cheeses over the beef. Add black beans, pickled jalapenos, diced red onions, diced tomatoes, and black olives.
5. For even cheesier nachos, layer half the chips and toppings, then repeat the second layer.
6. Bake for 8-10 minutes until the cheese is melted and bubbling.
7. Remove from oven and sprinkle with guacamole, sour cream, and chopped cilantro.
8. Mash ripe avocados with lime juice, salt, and garlic powder for a quick homemade guacamole. Serve immediately.
9. If you have leftovers (which is rare!), just reheat them in the oven to keep them crispy. They also make a great base for breakfast nachos - just add some scrambled eggs on top.

NUTRITIONAL INFO (PER SERVING):

Calories: 550, Carbohydrates: 42 g, Cholesterol: 70 mg, Sodium: 950 mg, Protein: 28 g, Fats: 32 g, Sugar: 3 g, Fiber: 6 g

Appetizers & Snacks

Poultry & Meat

LEMON CHICKEN WITH VEGETABLES

The main concern with roasting vegetables with proteins is to cook them evenly at the same time because these dishes are good warm. Cut the veggies the same size, and don't clutter the baking sheet so that the veggies and chicken will bake and brown well.
If you like crispy-crusted chicken like I do and you have the time, pan-fry it for the last 3-5 minutes of cooking, watching carefully to make sure it doesn't burn.

VARIATIONS:

Replace drumsticks with chicken thighs or breasts. Adjust cooking time as needed (breasts may take less time). Use whatever vegetables you prefer or have on hand, such as carrots, zucchini, or cherry tomatoes.

4 servings

15 minutes
(plus ½ hour to marinate)

35-40 minutes

INGREDIENTS:

CHICKEN DRUMSTICKS:

- 8 chicken drumsticks
- 2 tablespoons (30 ml) olive oil
- juice of 1 lemon
- zest of 1 lemon
- 1 lemon, thinly sliced
- 1 teaspoon (5 g) paprika
- 1 teaspoon (5 g) garlic powder
- 1 teaspoon (5 g) dried/fresh thyme
- Salt and pepper to taste

- a pinch of chili flakes/cayenne pepper (optional)

VEGETABLES:

- 2 cups (200 g) broccoli florets
- 1 cup (150 g) green beans, trimmed
- 1 cup (150 g) cauliflower florets
- 1 yellow bell pepper (150 g), sliced
- 1 tablespoon (15 ml) olive oil
- 1 teaspoon (5 g) dried/fresh oregano
- Salt and pepper to taste

HOW TO COOK:

1. Combine the olive oil, paprika, lemon juice, lemon zest, garlic powder, thyme, salt, and pepper.
2. Add the chicken drumsticks to the bowl and give them a good stir to coat them evenly with the marinade. Then, just cover and refrigerate for at least 30 minutes.
3. Preheat the oven to 400°F (200°C).
4. Place drumsticks on a sheet pan.
5. In another bowl, mix broccoli, green beans, cauliflower, and yellow bell pepper with olive oil, oregano, salt, and pepper.
6. Arrange the vegetables around the chicken pieces on a sheet pan.
7. Place lemon slices on top of the chicken drumsticks.
8. Bake for 35-40 minutes until the chicken pieces are cooked through and the vegetables are tender and lightly browned.
9. Halfway through cooking, turn the baking sheet over to ensure even cooking.
10. Remove from the oven and let rest for a few minutes before serving.
11. Serve hot, making sure there is a balanced portion of chicken and vegetables on each plate.

NUTRITIONAL INFO (PER SERVING):

Calories: 350, Carbohydrates: 12 g, Cholesterol: 110 mg, Sodium: 450 mg, Protein: 30 g, Fats: 20 g, Sugar: 4 g, Fiber: 4 g

BUFFALO CHICKEN STUFFED SWEET POTATOES

Stuffed sweet potatoes are convenient because they can be prepared ahead and assembled just before baking for a quick snack. For vegetarians, a version with cauliflower florets or roasted mushrooms instead of chicken would work well.

VARIATIONS:

Instead of store-bought buffalo sauce, you can make homemade sauce by combining ½ cup (120 ml) hot sauce (such as Frank's RedHot), ½ teaspoon Worcestershire sauce, ½ cup (120 ml) unsalted butter, 1 tablespoon white vinegar, ¼ teaspoon garlic powder, ¼ teaspoon cayenne pepper/chili powder/paprika, and ¼ teaspoon salt.

Whisk the mixture and simmer for about 5 minutes, stirring occasionally. Allow it to cool to room temperature.

4 servings   15 minutes   60 minutes

INGREDIENTS:

- 8 medium sweet potatoes
- 4 cups (500 g) shredded rotisserie chicken/beef/pork
- 1 cup (240 ml) buffalo sauce
- 2 cups (200 g) shredded cheddar cheese/crumbled blue cheese/ cheddar and mozzarella
- 1 cup (150 g) red onion, finely chopped
- 1 cup (240 ml) sour cream
- 1 cup (50 g) green onions, chopped
- 4 tablespoons (60 ml) olive oil
- Salt and pepper to taste

HOW TO COOK:

1. Preheat the oven to 400°F (200°C).
2. Pierce each potato around with a fork in several places.
3. Brush the sweet potato skins with olive oil and season with salt and pepper. Sweet potatoes should be evenly coated with olive oil for even roasting. Arrange them on a sheet pan.
4. Bake for 45-55 minutes until tender and can be easily pierced with a fork.
5. Let them cool slightly.
6. Meanwhile, mix the shredded fried chicken with the Buffalo sauce until well coated.
7. Make a slit down the center of each potato lengthwise and press the ends lightly to open them up.
8. Stuff each potato with the Buffalo chicken mixture.
9. Sprinkle the chicken with shredded cheddar cheese.
10. It's time to return the stuffed sweet potatoes to the oven. Bake them for about 10 to 15 minutes or until the cheese is melted and bubbling away.
11. Sprinkle finely chopped red onion and green onions on top.
12. Drizzle with sour cream before serving.

NUTRITIONAL INFO (PER SERVING):

Calories: 480, Carbohydrates: 50 g, Cholesterol: 85 mg, Sodium: 1250 mg, Protein: 28 g, Fats: 21 g, Sugar: 11 g, Fiber: 7 g

CHICKEN AND POTATOES

Make sure the chicken is evenly distributed on the sheet pan to ensure even cooking. If desired, it can be cut into two or more pieces. The lemon juice and zest, as well as the aromatic herbs, will give it a crispy crust. Sprinkle the chicken with the pan juices from time to time to keep it juicy and flavorful.

To make the potatoes crispy, you can boil them for 5-7 minutes before baking.

VARIATIONS:

For more variety, add carrots, bell peppers, or Brussels sprouts to the pan. For a savorier version, add a teaspoon of chili flakes to the herb mixture. Dried herbs can replace fresh herbs at a 1 to 3 ratio.

4 servings   20 minutes   60 minutes

INGREDIENTS:

- 1 whole chicken (4 lb./1.8 Kg)
- 2 lb. (900 g) baby potatoes
- ¼ cup (60 ml) olive oil
- 6 cloves garlic, minced
- 2 tablespoons fresh rosemary, chopped

- 1 tablespoon fresh thyme, chopped
- 1 tablespoon fresh oregano, chopped
- 1 lemon, zested and juiced
- 1 teaspoon salt
- ½ teaspoon black pepper

HOW TO COOK:

1. Preheat the oven to 400°F (200°C).
2. Pat the chicken dry with paper towels.
3. Combine the olive oil, crushed garlic, chopped rosemary, thyme, oregano, lemon zest, lemon juice, salt, and black pepper.
4. Rub the mixture all over the chicken, taking care to coat it evenly.
5. Wash and scrub the potatoes.
6. Coat the potatoes in the remaining herb mixture or, if needed, add a little more olive oil, salt, and pepper.
7. Place the chicken in the center of a sheet pan.
8. Arrange the potatoes around the chicken.
9. Bake for 60 minutes until the potatoes are golden and tender. Stir every 15 minutes. Check the readiness of the chicken by the internal temperature; it should be 165°F (74°C).
10. Let the chicken rest for 10 minutes before cutting.
11. Serve the chicken pieces with the baked potatoes.

NUTRITIONAL INFO (PER SERVING):

Calories: 620, Carbohydrates: 28 g, Cholesterol: 130 mg, Sodium: 600 mg, Protein: 46 g, Fats: 34 g, Sugar: 2 g, Fiber: 3 g

Poultry & Meat

CHICKEN WITH RAINBOW VEGETABLES

This is the most classic recipe for baking proteins with vegetables on a sheet pan. One such dish is worthy of dinner for the whole family. It is prepared very simply and quickly. However, dishes baked on a sheet pan usually turn out a bit dry and need a sauce.

My choices are lemon-garlic sauce, yogurt sauce with herbs, chimichurri sauce, tahini sauce, or honey mustard sauce. To give the cooked chicken and vegetables a bright flavor, pour the sauce over them just before serving.

VARIATIONS:

Replace chicken breasts with boneless chicken thighs, pork chops, or firm tofu for another protein source.

Depending on your preference and seasonal availability, use other vegetables such as zucchini, sweet potatoes, asparagus, or Brussels sprouts.

Spice up the dish with your favorite spices, such as cumin, curry powder, or Italian seasoning for a variety of flavors.

4 servings   15 minutes   25-30 minutes

INGREDIENTS:

- 2 large chicken breasts (1.5 lb./700 g)
- fresh parsley, for garnish

VEGETABLES:

- 2 large carrots (200 g), sliced
- 1 red bell pepper (150 g), chopped
- 1 yellow bell pepper (150 g), chopped
- 1 medium red onion (100 g), sliced
- 1 small head of broccoli (200 g), cut into florets

SEASONING:

- 2 tablespoons (30 ml) olive oil
- 1 teaspoon garlic powder
- 1 teaspoon paprika
- 1 teaspoon dried thyme
- 1 teaspoon salt
- ½ teaspoon black pepper

HOW TO COOK:

1. Preheat the oven to 400°F (200°C).
2. Mix the garlic powder, olive oil, paprika, dried thyme, salt, and black pepper.
3. Rub chicken breasts with half of the oil and herb mixture. For extra flavor, marinate chicken in seasoning mix and olive oil for at least 30 minutes or overnight before cooking.
4. Place the sliced carrots, red bell pepper, yellow bell pepper, red onion, and broccoli florets on a large baking sheet. Slice vegetables the same size to ensure even cooking.
5. Toss the vegetables with the remaining herb and oil mixture.
6. Place the seasoned chicken breasts in the center of the baking sheet.
7. Arrange the vegetables around the chicken.
8. Bake for 25-30 minutes until the chicken breasts are cooked through and the vegetables are soft. Stir every 15 minutes.
9. Slice chicken breasts and serve with roasted vegetables.
10. Garnish with fresh parsley if desired.

NUTRITIONAL INFO (PER SERVING):

Calories: 320, Carbohydrates: 18 g, Cholesterol: 85 mg, Sodium: 600 mg, Protein: 30 g, Fats: 12 g, Sugar: 7 g, Fiber: 6 g

TERIYAKI CHICKEN WITH PINEAPPLE

Baked chicken and vegetables go great with steamed jasmine rice, nutty-flavored brown rice, or rice noodles. Cook the rice with a little coconut milk to give it extra richness. For vegetable side dishes, consider roasted asparagus and bok choy.

If the Asian flair appeals to you, go for pineapple cake or mango sorbet for dessert.

VARIATIONS:

Substitute or add other vegetables, such as broccoli, carrots, or zucchini. This recipe can also be made with shrimp, tofu, or beef instead of chicken. Add a teaspoon of sriracha or chili flakes to the sauce for a spicier version.

4 servings   15 minutes   25 minutes

INGREDIENTS:

- 1 lb. (450 g) chicken breast, cut into bite-sized pieces
- 2 green onions, sliced (for garnish)

VEGETABLES:
- 1 red bell pepper (150 g), chopped
- 1 yellow bell pepper (150 g), chopped
- 1 cup (150 g) snap peas
- 1 cup (150 g) fresh/canned pineapple chunks, drained

SAUCE:
- ¼ cup (60 ml) soy sauce
- ¼ cup (60 ml) pineapple
- 2 tablespoons (30 ml) honey
- 1 tablespoon rice vinegar
- 1 tablespoon sesame oil
- 2 cloves garlic, minced
- 1 tablespoon fresh ginger, grated
- 1 tablespoon cornstarch with 2 tablespoons water (optional for thickening)

HOW TO COOK:

1. Preheat the oven to 425°F (220°C).
2. Arrange the chicken, bell peppers, peas, and pineapple chunks on a large sheet pan. Make sure the chicken and vegetables are cut into equal pieces for even cooking.
3. Mix the soy sauce, pineapple juice, honey, rice vinegar, sesame oil, garlic, and ginger. If you prefer a sharper flavor, use more pineapple juice and reduce the amount of honey.
4. Pour the sauce over the chicken chunks and vegetables. Stir to coat the vegetables evenly.
5. Bake for 20-25 minutes until the chicken pieces are cooked through and the vegetables are soft. If you want a thicker sauce, you can mix cornstarch with water and pour it over the chicken and vegetables halfway through baking.
6. Sprinkle with green onion before serving. Enjoy!
7. This dish makes great leftovers. Store in the fridge for up to 3 days. Reheat in the microwave or oven.

NUTRITIONAL INFO (PER SERVING):

Calories: 280, Carbohydrates: 25 g, Cholesterol: 55 mg, Sodium: 720 mg, Protein: 25 g, Fats: 10 g, Sugar: 15 g, Fiber: 3 g

Poultry & Meat

SAUSAGE WITH APPLES AND MUSTARD

The combination of sausages and apples is a classic pairing, dating back to traditional German and Central European cuisine. The sweet tartness of the apples perfectly complements the tangy, spicy flavor of the sausage. Roasting the sausages with apples and potatoes allows the natural sugars in the apples to caramelize.

This dish is easily adaptable to different dietary preferences. For a healthier version, use chicken or turkey sausage. For a vegetarian version, replace the sausages with plant-based alternatives or roasted chickpeas.

VARIATIONS:

Add various vegetables (bell peppers, carrots, or Brussels sprouts). Experiment with different spices (smoked paprika or cumin).

4 servings   15 minutes   30 minutes

INGREDIENTS:

- 4 sausages (Italian/bratwurst/chicken/turkey)
- 2 large apples (Honeycrisp/Granny Smith), sliced
- 1 lb. (450 g) potatoes, sliced (optional)
- 1 large onion, sliced

- 2 tablespoons whole-grain mustard
- 2 tablespoons olive oil
- 1 teaspoon dried thyme
- 1 teaspoon dried rosemary
- Salt and pepper to taste
- Fresh parsley, chopped (for garnish)

HOW TO COOK:

1. Preheat the oven to 400°F (200°C).
2. Arrange the sliced apples, potatoes, and onions on a large baking sheet. Make sure apple and potato slices are the same thickness for even cooking. To make the potatoes crispier, arrange them on a sheet pan so that they do not overlap.
3. Mix the olive oil, mustard, thyme, rosemary, salt, and pepper.
4. Drizzle the apples, potatoes, and onions with the dressing and stir to combine.
5. Place the sausages on top of the apple-potato mixture on a flat baking pan.
6. Bake for 25-30 minutes, flipping the sausages midway through cooking.
7. Sprinkle with fresh chopped parsley before serving.

NUTRITIONAL INFO (PER SERVING):

Calories: 450, Carbohydrates: 45 g, Cholesterol: 60 mg, Sodium: 800 mg, Protein: 20 g, Fats: 25 g, Sugar: 12 g, Fiber: 5 g

ROAST PORK WITH VEGETABLES

This recipe is perfect for both a weekend family dinner and a dinner party with friends. It is a lifesaver for holidays and special occasions, allowing you to create an impressive meal with minimal effort. Roast pork and vegetables can be the centerpiece dish for holiday feasts such as Christmas, Easter, or Thanksgiving. The recipe can easily be adapted to specific dietary needs by substituting vegetables or changing the seasonings.

I make it the weekend beforehand and spread it into lunch boxes for easy meals during the week.

VARIATIONS:

Marinating the pork before cooking in this recipe is optional, but if you have extra time and want to enhance the flavor and tenderness, marinating can be a great option.

Mix the olive oil, crushed garlic, dried thyme, dried rosemary, salt, and black pepper. Pour the marinade over the pork so that it is well coated. Place in the refrigerator for at least 1 hour, or preferably overnight. Continue cooking according to the recipe.

6 servings   20 minutes   1 hour 20 minutes

INGREDIENTS:

FOR THE PORK:

- 3.3 lb. (1.5 kg) boneless pork loin
- 2 Tbsp. (30 ml) olive oil
- 3 garlic cloves, minced
- 1 Tbsp. dried thyme
- 1 Tbsp. dried rosemary
- 1 tsp. salt
- ½ tsp. black pepper

FOR THE VEGETABLES:

- 4 medium carrots (300 g), sliced
- 4 medium beetroots (400 g), sliced
- 1 head broccoli (300 g), cut into florets
- 2 red bell peppers (300 g), sliced
- 2 Tbsp. (30 ml) olive oil
- 1 tsp. salt
- ½ tsp. black pepper
- 1 tsp. dried thyme
- 1 tsp. dried rosemary

HOW TO COOK:

1. Preheat the oven to 200°C (400°F).
2. Mix the olive oil, crushed garlic, dried thyme, dried rosemary, salt, and black pepper.
3. Rub this spicy mixture all over the pork tenderloin.
4. Cut vegetables into similar sizes to ensure they roast evenly. Toss the vegetables with olive oil, thyme, rosemary, salt, and pepper.
5. Use parchment paper for a sheet pan.
6. Place the carrots, beets, broccoli, and red bell pepper on a sheet pan.
7. Arrange the pork tenderloin in the center of a sheet pan, surrounded by the vegetables.
8. Bake for 70 - 80 minutes until the vegetables are tender and caramelized. Carefully stir the vegetables and pork every 15-20 minutes to ensure even roasting.
9. Check that the pork is cooked through with the meat thermometer. It should be 63°C (145°F).
10. Remove the sheet pan from the oven and let it rest for 10 minutes before slicing.
11. Slice the pork thinly and serve with roasted vegetables.

NUTRITIONAL INFO (PER SERVING):

Calories: 450, Carbohydrates: 18 g, Cholesterol: 110 mg, Sodium: 450 mg, Protein: 35 g, Fats: 25 g, Sugar: 8 g, Fiber: 6 g

BEEF FAJITAS

Fajitas originated in the 1930s on the Texas-Mexico border. It is a favorite dish in Tex-Mex cuisine, which combines Mexican and Texan culinary traditions. Ranch workers were often paid in meat scraps, such as skirt steak, which they marinated, grilled, and served with tortillas.

Fajitas can be cooked to your liking. Just adjust the spices to your preference, add different vegetables such as zucchini or mushrooms, and even substitute beef for chicken, shrimp, or vegetable protein. Tortillas can be made with corn or wheat flour.

VARIATIONS:

For more flavorful fajitas, marinate the beef in the seasoning mixture for at least 30 minutes before cooking. Vegetarians can substitute beef for portobello mushrooms or tofu. And cheese lovers sprinkle the fajitas with cheese in the last 5 minutes of baking.

54

4 servings   15 minutes   20 minutes

INGREDIENTS:

FOR THE FAJITAS:

- 1½ lb. (700 g) Beef Steak, sliced into thin strips
- 3 medium bell peppers (450 g) (red, yellow, green), sliced
- 1 large (100 g) white onion, sliced
- 3 Tbsp. (45 ml) olive oil
- 8 small tortillas, warmed
- ¼ cup fresh cilantro, for garnish
- lime wedges, for serving

FAJITA SEASONING MIX:

- 1 Tbsp. chili powder
- 1 tsp. ground cumin
- 1 tsp. paprika
- 1 tsp. garlic powder
- 1 tsp. onion powder
- ½ tsp. dried oregano
- 1 tsp. salt
- ½ tsp. black pepper

HOW TO COOK:

1. Preheat the oven to 400°F (200°C).
2. Combine the sliced beef, bell pepper, and onion. Make sure beef and vegetables are sliced evenly for even cooking.
3. Toss with olive oil and fajita seasoning mix. Stir everything together until well coated.
4. Arrange the beef and vegetable mixture evenly on a sheet pan.
5. Bake for 15-20 minutes, stirring halfway through, until the beef is cooked through and the vegetables are soft. Cooking over high heat helps to quickly caramelize the vegetables and brown the beef, enhancing their flavor.
6. Serve the beef and vegetables in warmed tortillas. Sprinkle with fresh cilantro leaves and a splash of lime juice.

NUTRITIONAL INFO (PER SERVING):

Calories: 450, Carbohydrates: 35 g, Cholesterol: 70 mg, Sodium: 900 mg, Protein: 28 g, Fats: 20 g, Sugar: 6 g, Fiber: 4 g

MEATLOAF AND MASHED POTATOES

Meatloaf and mashed potatoes are a staple of classic comfort food. It evokes a sense of nostalgia and warmth, awakening memories of family dinners and home-cooked meals.

The preparation of meatloaf made of minced meat, bread, and wine began as far back as ancient Rome. Different cultures have their versions of meatloaf. Germany has a similar dish called Hackbraten, and Italy has Polpettone, which is stuffed with eggs or ham. It became especially popular in America during the Great Depression as an economical way to supplement meat with breadcrumbs and vegetables.

VARIATIONS:

For a lighter version, substitute ground beef for ground turkey. Since you can add cheese to almost any dish and not go wrong, this recipe is no exception. 1 cup (120 g) of shredded cheddar cheese added to mashed potatoes gives it an extra tangy flavor.

6 servings   20 minutes   60 minutes

INGREDIENTS:

MEATLOAF:

- 2 lb. (900 g) ground beef
- 1 cup (240 ml) milk
- 1 cup (100 g) breadcrumbs
- 1 small onion, finely chopped
- 2 large eggs
- ¼ cup (60 ml) ketchup
- 2 Tbsp. (30 ml) Worcestershire sauce
- 1 tsp. salt
- ½ tsp. black pepper
- 1 tsp. garlic powder
- 1 tsp. dried thyme

GLAZE:

- 2 Tbsp. (30 g) brown sugar
- ½ cup (120 ml) ketchup/barbecue sauce/tomato sauce/mushroom gravy
- 1 Tbsp. (15 ml) Dijon mustard

MASHED POTATOES:

- 2 lb. (900 g) potatoes/sweet potatoes, peeled and cubed
- 1 cup (240 ml) milk
- ¼ cup (60 g) butter
- Salt and pepper to taste

VEGETABLES:

- 2 cups (300 g) broccoli florets/carrots/ bell peppers/green beans

HOW TO COOK:

1. Preheat oven to 375°F (190°C). Line a sheet pan with parchment paper.
2. Combine the ground beef, milk, breadcrumbs, chopped onion, eggs, ketchup, Worcestershire sauce, salt, black pepper, garlic powder, and dried thyme. Stir until thoroughly combined. If you like a finer texture, grind the mince in a food processor.
3. Form a loaf from the meat mixture and place it in the center of the sheet pan.
4. Mix your favorite ketchup, brown sugar, and Dijon mustard. Spread the glaze evenly over the meatloaf. Arrange the broccoli florets around the meatloaf on a sheet pan. Bake for about 60 minutes, or until the meatloaf is cooked through (internal temperature 160°F/70°C) and the broccoli is soft.
5. Let it rest for 10 minutes before slicing to preserve the juices.
6. Meanwhile, boil the cubed potatoes in salted water for 15-20 minutes until tender. You can also bake the cubed potatoes in foil in the oven along with the meatloaf.
7. Drain the water. Add the milk and butter. Purée the potatoes until smooth.
8. Serve the sliced meatloaf with mashed potatoes and broccoli.

NUTRITIONAL INFO (PER SERVING):

Calories: 520, Carbohydrates: 42 g, Cholesterol: 145 mg, Sodium: 980 mg, Protein: 30 g, Fats: 25 g, Sugar: 9 g, Fiber: 5 g

STUFFED BUTTERNUT SQUASH

Native Americans were eating squash long before European settlers arrived on the American continent. This healthy vegetable (or rather fruit) has been an essential part of the American diet for thousands of years. Roasting enhances its natural sweetness and gives it a caramelized flavor that pairs well with the spicy beef stuffing. Stuffed vegetables are a common dish in many cultures around the world. This recipe has similarities to Middle Eastern stuffed peppers, Greek hemistros (stuffed vegetables), and Mexican stuffed chilies. The stuffing can easily be varied with meat, beans, or grains.

VARIATIONS:

Replace ground beef with a mixture of black beans and quinoa for a vegetarian option. Sprinkle the stuffed zucchini with shredded cheese before final baking to give the dish a cheesy flavor.

4 servings   15 minutes   60 minutes

INGREDIENTS:

- 2 medium butternut squash, halved and de-seeded
- ¼ cup (35 g) pumpkin seeds
- Fresh parsley, chopped

FILLING:
- 1 lb. (450 g) ground beef
- 1 medium onion (70 g), diced
- 2 cloves garlic, minced
- 1 bell pepper (150 g), diced

- 1 cup (150 g) carrots, diced
- 1 can (15 oz/425 g) diced tomatoes
- diced jalapenos/a pinch of cayenne pepper (optional)
- 1 tsp. ground cumin
- 1 tsp. smoked paprika
- Salt and pepper, to taste
- 2 Tbsp. olive oil

HOW TO COOK:

1. Preheat the oven to 400°F (200°C).
2. Slice the squash flesh crosswise. Place the squash halves cut side up on a sheet pan. Drizzle with olive oil, salt, and pepper. Bake in the oven for 40 minutes until the flesh is tender. Flip the sheet pan halfway through the cooking time for even roasting.
3. Heat olive oil in a skillet over medium heat. Add the onion and fry for 3-5 minutes, stirring occasionally. Add garlic and cook for another minute.
4. Add ground beef to the fried onion and cook until browned, stirring occasionally. Add the diced bell peppers and carrots and cook for 5-7 minutes until the vegetables are soft.
5. Add jalapenos or cayenne pepper to the ground beef to spice up the dish, if desired.
6. Add the diced tomatoes, cumin, smoked paprika, salt and pepper. Simmer for about 10 minutes.
7. When the squash halves are soft, remove them from the oven. Scoop out some of the pulp, leaving ½ inch (1 cm) all around. Mix the pulp with the beef mixture.
8. Place the beef mixture in the hollowed-out squash halves. Sprinkle pumpkin seeds on top.
9. Return the stuffed zucchini to the oven and bake for another 20 minutes, until the stuffing is hot and the tops are slightly crispy.
10. Remove from the oven, garnish with fresh parsley, and serve hot.

NUTRITIONAL INFO (PER SERVING):

Calories: 350, Carbohydrates: 25 g, Cholesterol: 70 mg, Sodium: 300 mg, Protein: 25 g, Fats: 20 g, Sugar: 8 g, Fiber: 6 g

Poultry & Meat

PORK BELLY WITH VEGETABLES

Many cultures have their variations of roasted pork belly with vegetables. In the UK, pork belly is baked with apples and root vegetables, while in Germany, it is served with sauerkraut and potatoes.

Although pork belly contains a lot of fat, the key is to observe moderation. Spoil yourself without overdoing it. Combining it with a generous portion of vegetables will help soften the richness of the pork belly.

Adapt the recipe to seasonal vegetables. In the summer, bell peppers and zucchini can be used, while in the winter, root vegetables like parsnips and turnips are the perfect addition.

VARIATIONS:

Use soy sauce, hoisin sauce, and five-spice powder instead of olive oil, smoked paprika, and thyme to give the dish an Asian twist.
In the last 30 minutes of baking, brush the pork belly chunks with your favorite barbecue sauce for a sticky, sweet, and smoky flavor.

4 servings   20 minutes   90 minutes

- 2 lb. (900 g) pork belly, cut into thick slices
- 2 tsp. salt
- 1 tsp. black pepper
- 2 Tbsp. (30 ml) olive oil
- 1 tsp. smoked paprika
- 1 tsp. garlic powder
- 1 tsp. dried thyme

- Fresh rosemary sprigs for garnish
- 4 large carrots (400 g), chopped
- 2 large onions (200 g), quartered
- 2 leeks (200 g), sliced
- 4 garlic cloves, smashed
- 2 Tbsp. (30 ml) olive oil
- Salt and pepper, to taste

HOW TO COOK:

1. Preheat the oven to 375°F (190°C).
2. Cut the pork belly into thick chunks. Rub with salt, pepper, olive oil, smoked paprika, garlic powder, and dried thyme. You can bake the pork belly whole, but cutting it into chunks increases the surface area, allowing for more even cooking and a crispier crust.
3. In a large bowl, mix the carrots, onion, leeks, garlic, olive oil, salt, and pepper.
4. Arrange the seasoned vegetables evenly on a sheet pan.
5. Place the seasoned pork belly chunks on top of the vegetables on the sheet pan.
6. Bake for 90 minutes until the pork belly is crispy and the vegetables are tender. Turn the pork belly slices and flip the vegetables every 20 minutes to achieve even crispiness.
7. Garnish with sprigs of fresh rosemary.
8. Allow to rest for 8-10 minutes before serving.
9. Serve hot. Pork belly leftovers can be used in sandwiches, salads, or mixed fries.

NUTRITIONAL INFO (PER SERVING):

Calories: 850, Carbohydrates: 20 g, Cholesterol: 120 mg, Sodium: 950 mg, Protein: 15 g, Fats: 75 g, Sugar: 10 g, Fiber: 5 g

Poultry & Meat

Seafood

SALMON WITH VEGETABLES

I always say it's hard to mess up salmon. It is a lifesaver for any dish. Just make sure to check the place where it is caught to ensure it is sustainable. The nutrients and trace elements it contains contribute to heart and vascular health.

This recipe is incredibly versatile. You can substitute vegetables depending on the season or what you have on hand. Vegetables like zucchini, carrots, and Brussels sprouts are great alternatives. The marinade gives the recipe a bright flavor and a source of vitamin C.

VARIATIONS:

To make herb-crusted salmon, mix 1/4 cup (25 g) of finely chopped fresh herbs (parsley, dill, or basil) with the marinade.

4 servings   15 minutes   20-25 minutes

INGREDIENTS:

- 4 salmon fillets (6 oz./170 g each)
- Fresh thyme/parsley, for garnish
- sesame seeds (optional)

VEGETABLES:

- 1 bunch asparagus, trimmed
- 1 head broccoli (400 g), cut into florets
- 1 bell pepper (150 g), sliced (any color)
- 1 cup (150 g) cherry tomatoes, halved

MARINADE:

- 2 Tbsp. extra virgin olive oil/sesame oil
- 1 Tbsp. lemon juice
- 1 tsp. garlic powder
- 1 tsp. dried thyme
- Salt and black pepper, to taste

HOW TO COOK:

1. Preheat the oven to 400°F (200°C).
2. Arrange the asparagus, broccoli florets, bell pepper slices, and cherry tomato halves on a sheet pan.
3. Drizzle the vegetables with 1-2 tablespoons of olive oil (virgin olive oil preferred), salt and black pepper. Stir to coat the vegetables evenly.
4. Place the salmon fillets on top of the vegetables.
5. Whisk together 1 tablespoon olive oil, freshly squeezed lemon juice, garlic powder, dried thyme, salt, and pepper.
6. Spread the marinade evenly over the salmon fillets.
7. Bake for 20-25 minutes, or until the salmon fillets are cooked through and can be easily pierced with a fork and the vegetables are soft.
8. Before serving, let the salmon rest for a few minutes. Garnish with fresh greens or sesame seeds, if desired.

NUTRITIONAL INFO (PER SERVING):

Calories: 350, Carbohydrates: 10 g, Cholesterol: 70 mg, Sodium: 250 mg, Protein: 35 g, Fats: 20 g, Sugar: 5 g, Fiber: 4 g

Seafood

CAJUN SHRIMP BOIL

Cajun cuisine originated in rural Louisiana and was brought by the Acadians, French settlers who were expelled from Canada. Andouille sausage is a smoked pork sausage native to France. The inclusion of corn and potatoes reflects the influence of Native American and European cuisines on Cajun cuisine.

Cajun seasoning includes a blend of spices such as paprika, cayenne nut, garlic powder, onion powder, and oregano. This combination gives the dish a rich flavor that is both tangy and spicy at the same time.

Boiled shrimp is a dish that is often served at parties and gatherings. It is perfect for sharing with friends and family, creating a casual and festive atmosphere.

VARIATIONS:

If you like a greater variety of vegetables, add bell peppers and white or red onions. You can also experiment with different seafood, such as crab legs or mussels.

6 servings   15 minutes   30 minutes

INGREDIENTS:

- 2 lb. (900 g) large shrimp, deveined and shell-on/peeled
- 1½ lb. (680 g) baby red potatoes, halved
- 3 ears corn on the cob, cut into thirds
- 12 oz. (340 g) Andouille sausage, sliced

- ½ cup (120 ml) butter, melted/olive oil
- 4 garlic cloves, minced
- 3 Tbsp. Cajun seasoning
- fresh parsley, chopped, for garnish
- 1 lemon, cut into wedges

HOW TO COOK:

1. Preheat the oven to 400°F (200°C).
2. Combine the potatoes, corn, 2 tablespoons of melted butter, and 1.5 tablespoons of Cajun seasoning. Stir.
3. Arrange the potatoes and corn on a large sheet pan. Bake for 20 minutes.
4. After 20 minutes, add sausage and shrimp to the sheet pan. Drizzle with the remaining melted butter and Cajun seasoning, and add the minced garlic. Stir gently so everything is evenly coated.
5. Return to the oven and bake for another 10 minutes or until the shrimp are opaque and pink.
6. Shrimp cook very quickly, usually within a few minutes. So, cook the potatoes and corn first, and add the shrimp at the end so that everything is ready.
7. Remove from the oven and serve on the sheet pan. Garnish with fresh parsley and lemon wedges.

NUTRITIONAL INFO (PER SERVING):

Calories: 450, Carbohydrates: 32 g, Cholesterol: 285 mg, Sodium: 1280 mg, Protein: 30 g, Fats: 24 g, Sugar: 4 g, Fiber: 4 g

Seafood

BAKED COD WITH TOMATOES

You can use different types of fish for this recipe. Here are some great alternatives: haddock (similar in texture and flavor to cod), halibut (firm, meaty fish that holds up well during baking and pairs with tomatoes and olives), tilapia (has a mild flavor and tender texture), pollock (is a good substitute for cod, with a slightly firmer texture), snapper (red snapper gives a slightly sweet flavor to the dish), sea bass (has a rich flavor and firm texture), mahi-mahi (has a firm texture suitable for baking), grouper (a mild but flavorful fish with a firm texture).

When substituting fish, make sure the fillets are the same thickness as the cod to ensure even cooking time. If the fish is significantly thicker or thinner than the cod fillet, alter the baking time slightly.

VARIATIONS:

Add capers and a little white wine before baking to give the dish an extra Mediterranean flavor. For a spicy touch, sprinkle with red pepper flakes or finely chopped fresh chili.

4 servings   10 minutes   20 minutes

INGREDIENTS:

- 4 cod fillets (6 oz./170 g each)
- 2 cups (300 g) cherry tomatoes, halved
- 1 cup (150 g) green olives, pitted and sliced
- 2 Tbsp. olive oil
- 2 cloves garlic, minced

- 1 tsp. dried oregano/fresh basil
- 1 tsp. dried thyme/fresh dill
- ½ tsp. salt
- ¼ tsp. black pepper
- 1 lemon, sliced
- Fresh parsley, chopped (for garnish)

HOW TO COOK:

1. Preheat the oven to 400°F (200°C).
2. Line a sheet pan with parchment paper or lightly grease it with olive oil.
3. Arrange the cod fillets on the sheet pan. Or you can marinate them for 30 minutes before baking to give them an extra depth of flavor.
4. Drizzle the fillets with 1 tablespoon of olive oil. Sprinkle evenly with the minced garlic, dried oregano, dried thyme, salt, and black pepper.
5. Spread the cherry tomatoes and green olives around and on top of the cod fillets.
6. Drizzle the tomatoes and olives with the remaining 1 tablespoon of olive oil.
7. Place the lemon slices on top of the cod.
8. Bake for 15-20 minutes or until the cod is opaque and can be easily pierced with a fork. Keep an eye on the cod near the end of baking to ensure it doesn't dry out.
9. Garnish with chopped fresh parsley and serve.

NUTRITIONAL INFO (PER SERVING):

Calories: 240, Carbohydrates: 6 g, Cholesterol: 70 mg, Sodium: 460 mg, Protein: 30 g, Fats: 10 g, Sugar: 2 g, Fiber: 2 g

FISH AND CHIPS

The first fish and chip (chippy) shop opened in London or Lancashire in the 1860s. The dish became a staple food for workers due to its ease of preparation.

Although fish and chips are traditionally deep-fried, baking is a healthier alternative as it reduces the amount of oil. This option maintains the crispy texture but has fewer calories and fat.

Fish and chips are traditionally served with malt vinegar, tartar sauce, and mushy peas. In Scotland, a popular addition is 'chippy sauce', a mixture of brown sauce and vinegar.

VARIATIONS:

For an herbal flavor, add 1 tablespoon chopped fresh herbs (dill, parsley, or thyme) to the batter. For a savory crust, add 1/2 teaspoon of cayenne pepper to the chip seasoning.

4 servings   15 minutes   25 minutes

INGREDIENTS:

FOR THE CHIPS:

- 4 large russet potatoes 2 lb./900 g), peeled and cut into wedges
- 2 Tbsp. (30 ml) olive oil
- 1 tsp. salt
- ½ tsp. black pepper
- ½ tsp. paprika

FOR THE FISH:

- 4 white fish fillets (cod/haddock/pollock/whiting can), (6 oz./170 g each)

- 1 cup (120 g) all-purpose flour/whole-grain flour/gluten-free flour
- 1 tsp. baking powder
- 1 tsp. salt
- ½ tsp. black pepper
- 1 cup (240 ml) cold beer
- 1 whole egg, beaten
- Oil spray
- Lemon wedges, for garnish
- Fresh parsley, chopped

HOW TO COOK:

1. Preheat the oven to 425°F (220°C).
2. Put the potato wedges in a bowl and coat with olive oil, salt, black pepper and paprika. For crispier chips, soak the potato wedges in cold water for ½ hour before baking to remove excess starch.
3. Arrange the wedges on a sheet pan in a single layer.
4. Bake for 12-16 minutes until golden and crispy. Turn once.
5. Mix all-purpose flour, baking powder, salt, and black pepper in a bowl.
6. Whisk in the cold beer and beaten egg until the batter is smooth. Make sure the beer is cold to make the batter light and crisp. Using beer allows for a lighter and crispier texture at the expense of carbonation.
7. Dip each fish fillet into the batter, letting the excess drip off.
8. Place the fish fillets in the batter on a sheet pan with the potatoes, being careful not to touch.
9. Continue baking for 10-15 minutes until the fish is golden and cooked through. Flip the potato wedges and fish fillets halfway through.
10. Garnish with lemon slices and fresh parsley. Serve hot.

NUTRITIONAL INFO (PER SERVING):

Calories: 480, Carbohydrates: 55 g, Cholesterol: 75 mg, Sodium: 900 mg, Protein: 28 g, Fats: 15 g, Sugar: 2 g, Fiber: 5 g

Seafood

Vegetables & Sides

BAKED TOMATOES WITH CHEESE

Cherry tomatoes are known for their sweet and juicy flavor, making them ideal for roasting. Baking intensifies their natural sweetness and lightly caramelizes them. Roasting with garlic and herbs infuses the flavors into the tomatoes and cheese, resulting in a rich and flavorful dish. Roasting the garlic softens its intense aroma and imparts a sweet and nutty flavor.

Choose any soft cheese suitable for melting. Feta, burrata, mozzarella, halloumi or similar are suitable. They can get a golden crust and melt slightly when baked, giving flavor and texture to the dish.

VARIATIONS:

Add other roasted vegetables such as zucchini, bell peppers, or red onions. A pinch of red pepper flakes will spice up the dish. Roasting the garlic softens its flavor. Roasted garlic can be squeezed out of its skin and mixed with the feta and tomatoes.

4 servings   10 minutes   30 minutes

INGREDIENTS:

- 2 lb. (900 g) cherry tomatoes
- 1 block (8 oz./225 g) feta cheese/2 balls burrata cheese (8 oz./225 g each)/mozzarella
- 1 head garlic, halved crosswise
- 2 Tbsp. olive oil

- 1 tsp. dried oregano
- 1 tsp. dried thyme
- Salt and pepper, to taste
- Fresh thyme sprigs, for garnish

HOW TO COOK:

1. Preheat the oven to 400°F (200°C).
2. Place the cherry tomatoes and the garlic head cut in half on a sheet pan.
3. Arrange a block of feta cheese in the center of the tomatoes and garlic.
4. Drizzle the tomatoes, garlic, and feta with olive oil.
5. Sprinkle everything with dried oregano, dried thyme, salt, and pepper.
6. Bake for about 30 minutes until the feta is golden brown.
7. Garnish with sprigs of fresh thyme.
8. Serve warm with a simple green salad, pasta or as a topping for toasted bread.

NUTRITIONAL INFO (PER SERVING):

Calories: 320, Carbohydrates: 12 g, Cholesterol: 35 mg, Sodium: 600 mg, Protein: 7 g, Fats: 16 g, Sugar: 8 g, Fiber: 3 g

Vegetables & Sides

RED CABBAGE WITH APPLES

The combination of red cabbage and apples is a classic in many traditional cuisines, such as German, Scandinavian, and Eastern European cuisines. Each culture adds its unique twist, such as different spices, herbs, or additional ingredients like bacon or sausage. The sweetness of the apples balances the slightly bitter and earthy flavor of the cabbage.

This dish pairs well with a variety of main dishes, including baked meats, grilled fish, or vegetarian dishes. It is a versatile side dish that can complement both simple and elaborate dishes.

VARIATIONS:

For more variety, add sliced carrots or sweet potatoes to the pan. Vegans can use a vegan alternative to cheese. If you are using fresh thyme, sprinkle the cabbage and apples with whole sprigs before baking.

4 servings   15 minutes   25 minutes

INGREDIENTS:

- 1 head red cabbage (800 g), sliced into ½ inch (1 cm) thick rounds
- 2 apples (Gala, Fuji), cored and sliced
- olive oil spray
- salt and ground lemon pepper, to taste

- 1 tsp. salt
- 1 tsp. dried thyme
- ½ cup (60 g) walnuts, chopped/ sunflower seeds
- ½ cup (60 g) cheddar cheese/goat cheese, grated
- 1 Tbsp. lemon juice, for sprinkling

HOW TO COOK:

1. Spray cabbage wedges and apple slices with olive oil and sprinkle with salt, thyme, and lemon pepper. Make sure you season both sides.
2. Preheat your oven to 400°F (205°C). Arrange cabbage wedges and apples in a single layer on a sheet pan (pre-lined with parchment paper). Bake for 20 minutes until slightly browned. Flip once halfway through.
3. Remove the sheet pan with cabbage from the oven and sprinkle the chopped walnuts and grated cheddar cheese over the cabbage and apples.
4. Roast for an additional 5-10 minutes, until the cheese is melted and the walnuts are lightly toasted.
5. Transfer roasted cabbage and apples to a serving plate and sprinkle with lemon juice.

NUTRITIONAL INFO (PER SERVING):

Calories: 220, Total Fat: 18 g, Chol: 10 mg, Sodium: 300 mg, Total Carbs: 15 g, Fiber: 4 g, Total Sugars: 8 g, Protein: 5 g

PUMPKIN WITH FIGS

The sweet and salty flavors of baked pumpkin and figs pair perfectly with roasted chicken, grilled lamb, or pork. If you add wild rice, quinoa, or farro and stir, you can have a whole meal. The grain's nutty flavor balances the softness of roasted vegetables.

A fresh arugula salad with a light lemon vinaigrette adds freshness to the rich flavor of roasted vegetables. A spinach and goat cheese salad balances the sweetness of figs and pumpkin due to the tartness of the goat cheese and the earthiness of the spinach.

VARIATIONS:

Add a little nutmeg or cloves for a warmer, spicier flavor. For a different flavor, replace figs with pears or apples. Sprinkle with toasted pecans or walnuts to give the dish a crunch.

4 servings   15 minutes   40 minutes

INGREDIENTS:

- 1 small pumpkin/butternut squash (2 lb./900 g), peeled and deseeded
- 4-5 fresh figs, halved
- 2 medium red onions (140 g), quartered
- 2 Tbsp. olive oil
- 1 tsp. salt

- ½ tsp. black pepper
- ½ tsp. ground cinnamon
- 1 Tbsp. maple syrup/honey (optional)
- Fresh herbs (sage, thyme) for garnish
- Edible flowers for garnish (optional)

HOW TO COOK:

1. Preheat the oven to 400°F (200°C). Line a sheet pan with parchment paper.
2. Slice the pumpkin into slices about 1/2 inch (1 cm) thick.
3. Place the pumpkin slices, fig halves, and red onion quarters on a sheet pan.
4. Drizzle with olive oil, black pepper, salt, and ground cinnamon. Gently stir to combine.
5. Bake for 35-40 minutes until the pumpkin is tender and the edges are lightly caramelized.
6. During the last 10 minutes of baking, drizzle the pumpkin with maple syrup or honey.
7. For additional caramelization, increase oven temperature to 425°F (220°C) for the last 10 minutes.
8. Garnish with fresh herbs and edible flowers.
9. Serve warm.

NUTRITIONAL INFO (PER SERVING):

Calories: 240, Carbohydrates: 6 g, Cholesterol: 70 mg, Sodium: 460 mg, Protein: 30 g, Fats: 10 g, Sugar: 2 g, Fiber: 2 g

Vegetables & Sides

VEGETABLE TART

I've provided a recipe for a tart with pre-made puff pastry. But if you have time, you can prepare it yourself. The dough recipe includes simple ingredients. For this tart, you need 2½ cups all-purpose flour, 1 cup (120 g) cold butter (small cubes), ½ cup (120 ml) cold water, ½ teaspoon salt, and 1 teaspoon fresh lemon juice (optional). Knead the dough to a homogeneous texture, roll it out, wrap it in plastic wrap, and put it in the refrigerator. Repeat several times. It takes a whole day for me, so I prefer to buy ready-made dough.

VARIATIONS:

To give the dish a Mediterranean flavor, add olives and feta cheese instead of regular cheese. Meat lovers can add slices of cooked bacon or ham on top of the vegetables before baking.

8 servings   20 minutes   40 minutes

INGREDIENTS:

- 1 sheet puff pastry (10x15 inches/ 25x38 cm)
- 2 Tbsp. olive oil
- 1 large onion (100 g), thinly sliced
- 3 carrots (250 g), diced
- 1 cup (150 g) cherry tomatoes, halved

- 1 bell pepper (150 g), sliced
- 2 cups (200 g) grated cheese (mozzarella/cheddar/gruyere)
- 2 cloves garlic, minced
- Salt and pepper to taste
- 1 tsp. dried thyme
- fresh parsley/basil for garnish

HOW TO COOK:

1. Preheat the oven to 400°F (200°C). Line a sheet pan with parchment paper.
2. Roll out the puff pastry and place it inside the sheet pan. Pierce the dough with a fork so it doesn't puff up too much during baking.
3. For a crispier base, pre-bake the puff pastry for 10 minutes before adding the filling.
4. Heat olive oil in a frying pan over low-medium heat. Fry the chopped onion for 3-5 minutes until it begins to soften. Add the carrots, bell pepper, and garlic. Cook for 10 minutes until the vegetables are soft, stirring occasionally.
5. Spread the sautéed vegetables evenly over the prepared puff pastry. Arrange the cherry tomatoes on top. Sprinkle the vegetables with grated cheese. Season with dried thyme, salt, and pepper.
6. Bake for 20-25 minutes until the dough is golden brown and the cheese is melted and bubbling.
7. Let cool for a few minutes. Sprinkle with fresh herbs before serving.

NUTRITIONAL INFO (PER SERVING):

Calories: 250, Carbohydrates: 20 g, Cholesterol: 25 mg, Sodium: 300 mg, Protein: 8 g, Fats: 15 g, Sugar: 5 g, Fiber: 3 g

Vegetables & Sides

VEGGIE MEDLEY

This recipe helps me out in any situation where I need to make a quick meal for a whole family or a company of friends. It's a transformer recipe – you can substitute these vegetables for any other ones you have in the fridge. If you add grains or chickpeas, it makes a complete vegetarian dinner. And if you add chicken, sausages, ham, or pieces of meat, this dish will be to the taste of meat-eaters.

VARIATIONS:

Add canned chickpeas (drained and rinsed) to add protein. Cayenne pepper or red pepper flakes will spice things up.

4 servings   15 minutes   35 minutes

INGREDIENTS:

- 4 medium sweet potatoes (600 g/ 1.3 lb.), thinly sliced but not all the way through (Hasselback style)
- 10 oz. (600 g) broccoli florets
- 2 medium (300 g/10 oz.)zucchini, sliced into rounds
- 4 oz. (100 g) baby arugula (Rocket)
- 4 oz. (100 g) radicchio, roughly chopped
- 2 Tbsp. (30 ml) olive oil
- 1 tsp. salt

- 1 tsp. black pepper
- 1 tsp. garlic powder
- 1 tsp. paprika
- 2 Tbsp. fresh chives, chopped

FOR THE TAHINI SAUCE:
- 3 Tbsp. tahini
- 2 Tbsp. lemon juice
- 2 Tbsp. water
- 1 garlic clove, minced
- ½ tsp. salt

HOW TO COOK:

1. Preheat the oven to 200°C (400°F). Don't forget to line a sheet pan with parchment paper.
2. Put the sweet potatoes on a cutting board. With a sharp knife, make thin slices across each potato, cutting almost to the bottom but not through. Place the prepared sweet potatoes on a large sheet pan.
3. Arrange the broccoli florets, zucchini circles, and sliced radicchio around the sweet potatoes on the sheet pan.
4. Drizzle the vegetables with olive oil. Sprinkle with garlic powder, paprika, salt, and black pepper. Gently stir the vegetables to coat evenly.
5. Bake for 25-35 minutes until the sweet potatoes are tender and the edges are crisp. Stir the vegetables midway through the cooking time for even roasting.
6. Whisk together the tahini, lemon juice, water, minced garlic, and salt until smooth. Add more water if necessary to achieve the desired consistency.
7. Serve the vegetables over a bed of baby arugula. Drizzle with tahini sauce and garnish with chopped fresh chives.

NUTRITIONAL INFO (PER SERVING):

Calories: 230, Carbohydrates: 40 g, Cholesterol: 0 mg, Sodium: 400 mg, Protein: 6 g, Fats: 8 g, Sugar: 9 g, Fiber: 8 g

Vegetables & Sides

MAC AND CHEESE WITH BRUSSELS SPROUTS

Macaroni and cheese is the king of side dishes in our family. This truly comfort food is so delicious that I build my entire dinner around it. I pick and choose which meats or vegetables go well with it, but it still tops them all. Even people who don't like pasta love it.

This dish is very simple to prepare: make a béchamel sauce, add spices and cheese, add the pasta, and bake in the oven until golden. If you add cooked bacon, ham, or shredded chicken to the pasta, you'll have a complete dinner.

VARIATIONS:

To spice up the dish, add 1-2 teaspoons of pepper sauce or a bit of cayenne pepper to the cheese sauce. You can also add other roasted vegetables, such as bell peppers, zucchini, or broccoli, to the Brussels sprouts. Feel free to mix and match different types of cheese depending on your preference. Gruyere, fontina, and Gouda are great alternatives.

8 servings   20 minutes   30 minutes

INGREDIENTS:

MAC AND CHEESE:

- 1 lb. (450 g) elbow macaroni, cooked al dente
- 4 cups (1 L) whole milk
- ½ cup (120 ml) heavy cream (double cream)
- ½ cup (65 g) all-purpose flour (plain flour)
- ½ cup (113 g) unsalted butter
- 4 cups (400 g) sharp cheddar cheese, shredded
- 2 cups (200 g) mozzarella cheese, shredded
- 1 cup (100 g) Parmesan cheese, grated
- 1 tsp. garlic powder
- 1 tsp. onion powder
- Salt and black pepper to taste

BRUSSELS SPROUTS:

- 1 lb. (450 g) Brussels sprouts, trimmed and halved
- 2 Tbsp. (30 ml) olive oil
- Salt and black pepper to taste

TOPPING:

- 1 cup (120 g) panko breadcrumbs
- 2 Tbsp. unsalted butter, melted
- ½ cup (50 g) Parmesan, grated

HOW TO COOK:

1. Preheat the oven to 375°F (190°C).
2. Toss the Brussels sprout halves with olive oil, salt, and pepper. Spread them on a sheet pan. Bake for 15-20 minutes until soft and golden, flipping once.
3. Add flour to the saucepan with melted butter. Cook over medium heat for 1-2 minutes until lightly golden, stirring constantly.
4. Gradually pour in the milk and cream, stirring constantly, until the mixture thickens and bubbles.
5. Remove from heat and add the sharp cheddar, mozzarella, parmesan, garlic powder, and onion powder. Season with salt and pepper to taste.
6. Combine cooked pasta, roasted Brussels sprouts, and cheese sauce. Mix well.
7. Spread the pasta mixture evenly in a sheet pan.
8. Mix the panko breadcrumbs, melted butter, and parmesan cheese in a bowl. Sprinkle evenly over the macaroni and cheese.
9. Bake for 20-25 minutes or until golden brown and crispy. For an even crispier filling, broil the macaroni and cheese in the last 2-3 minutes of baking.
10. Let it cool slightly before serving. Enjoy the pasta with Brussels sprouts in the pan!

NUTRITIONAL INFO (PER SERVING):

Calories: 650, Carbohydrates: 65 g, Cholesterol: 105 mg, Sodium: 800 mg, Protein: 25 g, Fats: 35 g, Sugar: 8 g, Fiber: 4 g

Vegetables & Sides

ROASTED VEGETABLES

Roasted veggies are a great, versatile side dish that's also really healthy! It is very easy to prepare. My family likes the vegetables to be almost raw, slightly softened but crispy and caramelized. So, I place the vegetables on the sheet pan as they are ready. Root vegetables first, then the softer peppers and zucchini. Young seasonal vegetables are great for this kind of baking. The vegetarians in our family eat roasted vegetables as a separate dish, and I serve them as a side dish to chicken, fish, or meat. Sometimes, I can roast them together.

VARIATIONS:

To give the dish some heat, add chili flakes or cayenne pepper to the seasoning. Feel free to use other vegetables, such as sweet potatoes, broccoli, or Brussels sprouts. Experiment with different herbs (rosemary, oregano, or basil).

4 servings   15 minutes   35 minutes

INGREDIENTS:

VEGETABLES:

- 1 lb. (450 g) baby carrots
- 1 lb. (450 g) baby beets
- 2 bell peppers (250 g), sliced
- 1 cup (4 oz/100 g) mushrooms, halved
- 1 zucchini (8 oz/225 g), sliced

SEASONING:

- 3 Tbsp. olive oil
- 1 tsp. salt
- ½ tsp. black pepper
- 1 tsp. garlic powder
- 1 tsp. smoked paprika
- 1 tsp. dried thyme
- 1 Tbsp. lemon zest

FOR SERVING:

- 1 cup (240 ml) hummus
- Fresh herbs (thyme, parsley) for garnish

HOW TO COOK:

1. Preheat the oven to 425°F (220°C).
2. Place all the vegetables in a large bowl. Add olive oil, salt, pepper, garlic powder, smoked paprika, dried thyme, and lemon zest. Stir to make sure all the vegetables are evenly coated.
3. Arrange the seasoned vegetables on a sheet pan in a single layer. Bake for 25-35 minutes until tender and lightly caramelized, stirring midway through cooking.
4. Remove from oven and let cool slightly. Serve with hummus on the side and garnish with fresh herbs.

NUTRITIONAL INFO (PER SERVING):

Calories: 200, Carbohydrates: 26 g, Cholesterol: 0 mg, Sodium: 420 mg, Protein: 4 g, Fats: 10 g, Sugar: 11 g, Fiber: 7 g

Vegetables & Sides

ROASTED POTATOES AND GREEN BEANS

Arrange the vegetables in a single layer, without overcrowding the sheet pan, so that they are well roasted and not steamed. Roasting at high temperatures helps caramelize the vegetables, bringing out their natural sweetness. Stir the vegetables midway through the roasting process to ensure they roast evenly and develop a beautiful color.

VARIATIONS:

Sprinkle ¼ cup (25 g) grated parmesan cheese over the vegetables in the last 5 minutes of baking to give the dish a cheesy flavor. Add 1 tablespoon (15 ml) lemon juice and the zest of 1 lemon to the vegetables before baking for a fresh, tangy flavor.

4 servings   15 minutes   35 minutes

INGREDIENTS:

- 1 lb. (450 g) fingerling potatoes, halved lengthwise
- 1 lb. (450 g) green beans, trimmed
- 2 Tbsp. olive oil
- 1 tsp. salt

- ½ tsp. black pepper
- 1 tsp. garlic powder
- 1 tsp. dried thyme/rosemary/oregano
- 1 tsp. paprika

HOW TO COOK:

1. Preheat the oven to 425°F (220°C).
2. In a large bowl, combine the potatoes and green beans with the olive oil, salt, black pepper, garlic powder, dried thyme, and paprika. Stir to make sure all the vegetables are evenly coated.
3. Place the seasoned vegetables in a single layer on a sheet pan.
4. Bake for 35-40 minutes until the potatoes are tender and lightly browned, stirring throughout the cooking time.
5. Remove from the oven and serve immediately.

NUTRITIONAL INFO (PER SERVING):

Calories: 170, Carbohydrates: 29 g, Cholesterol: 0 mg, Sodium: 400 mg, Protein: 4 g, Fats: 6 g, Sugar: 4 g, Fiber: 6 g

Vegetables & Sides

EGGPLANT PARMESAN

Eggplant parmesan, or parmigiana di melanzane, is a classic dish from the South of Italy that has been made since the 18th century.

Tomatoes are eggplant's natural companion in this dish. The acidity of the tomatoes balances the slightly bitter flavor of the eggplant. Mozzarella and Parmesan cheeses are traditional options for Eggplant Parmesan. Mozzarella provides a creamy, melting texture, while Parmesan provides a sharp, tangy flavor. The traditional technique for cooking eggplant is to sprinkle it with salt before cooking to reduce bitterness and remove excess moisture. This procedure makes the eggplants tender rather than soggy. You can vary the recipe by adding prosciutto, ham, or different types of cheese.

VARIATIONS:

Vegans can use vegan cheese alternatives. Add red pepper flakes to the layers to spice things up. Use a freshly grated mozzarella and parmesan mixture for better flavor and texture. This kind of cheese melts better and has a superior flavor compared to pre-shredded varieties.

6 servings   20 minutes   40 minutes

INGREDIENTS:

- 2 medium eggplants, sliced
- 4 medium tomatoes, sliced
- 2 cups (480 ml) marinara sauce
- 1 cup (200 g) mozzarella, shredded
- 1 cup (100 g) Parmesan, grated
- 1 cup breadcrumbs
- 1 lemon zest

- 5 Tbsp. olive oil, divided
- 1 tsp. dried oregano
- 1 tsp. dried basil
- ½ tsp. garlic powder
- ½ tsp. salt
- ¼ tsp. black pepper
- Fresh basil leaves, for garnish

HOW TO COOK:

1. Preheat the oven to 400°F (200°C).
2. Gently place the eggplant slices in a single layer on a wire rack and sprinkle with a little salt. Leave them for 20 minutes to draw out excess moisture. Pat them dry with paper towels.
3. Heat 2-3 tablespoons of olive oil in a skillet over medium heat. Add breadcrumbs and fry for 5-6 minutes until lightly browned, stirring constantly. Add the garlic powder, lemon zest, basil, and oregano. Cook for 1-2 minutes, stirring frequently.
4. Spread marinara sauce on the sheet pan. Layer eggplant slices on top of the sauce. Drizzle with olive oil and sprinkle with salt and pepper. Bake for 5 minutes on each side.
5. Take the sheet pan out of the oven and place the tomato slices among the eggplant slices.
6. Sprinkle with the mixture of shredded mozzarella and grated parmesan. Top everything with the breadcrumb mixture.
7. Bake for 15-20 minutes until the cheese is melted and bubbling.
8. Garnish the dish with fresh basil leaves before serving.

NUTRITIONAL INFO (PER SERVING):

Calories: 250, Carbohydrates: 15 g, Cholesterol: 40 mg, Sodium: 600 mg, Protein: 14 g, Fats: 15 g, Sugar: 8 g, Fiber: 6 g

Vegetables & Sides

This soft Italian flatbread is very similar to pizza. With pizza, we focus on the toppings, while focaccia is dough-centered. The result is perfect, whatever sweet or savory topping you add. I tasted it with olives, grated hard cheese, mozzarella, sliced pears, and onion rings. I have baked one big flatbread and many small "focaccini." It pairs with any dip, soup, salad, or shakshuka.

VARIATIONS:

Herb focaccia: Replace the onion and feta with fresh herbs (rosemary, basil, and oregano). Sprinkle generously with grated parmesan cheese on top before baking.

Focaccia with tomatoes and olives: Before baking, add halved cherry tomatoes and sliced olives on top of the dough. Sprinkle with dried oregano and sea salt.

Garlic and rosemary focaccia: Add crushed garlic and fresh rosemary to the olive oil. Brush the oil onto the dough with a brush and sprinkle with sea salt.

12 servings   20 minutes   30 minutes
(plus 2 hours for rising)

INGREDIENTS:

DOUGH

- 4 cups (480 g) all-purpose flour
- 2 tsp. salt
- 1 tsp. sugar
- 2¼ tsp. active dry yeast
- 1½ cups (360 ml) warm water
- ¼ cup (60 ml) olive oil, plus more for drizzling

TOPPINGS

- 1 large onion (120 g), thinly sliced
- ¼ cup (60 ml) olive oil
- 1 cup (150 g) feta cheese, crumbled
- 1 Tbsp. fresh thyme
- Salt and pepper, to taste

HOW TO COOK:

1. Mix the flour, salt, and sugar.
2. Dissolve the yeast in the warm water and let it foam for 5 minutes.
3. Add the yeast and 1/4 cup (60 ml) olive oil to the flour mixture. Knead until the dough forms.
4. Sprinkle the surface lightly with flour and knead the dough until smooth and elastic. This usually takes 8 to 10 minutes.
5. Leave the dough to rise, covered with a damp cloth. It will double in size in about 1 to 2 hours. The dough rises well in a warm, draft-free room. If the kitchen is cold, you can put the dough in the oven with the light on to allow it to rise.
6. Meanwhile, heat 1/4 cup (60 ml) olive oil in a skillet over medium heat.
7. Fry the onion slices, stirring occasionally, until caramelized, about 10-15 minutes. Set it aside.
8. Preheat the oven to 425°F (220°C).
9. Grease a sheet pan with olive oil.
10. Punch down the risen dough and transfer it to the prepared sheet pan. Stretch and press the dough against the sheet pan.
11. Make indentations all over the dough.
12. Spread the caramelized onion slices evenly over the dough.
13. Sprinkle the onions with crumbled feta cheese and fresh thyme leaves.
14. Season the focaccia with salt and pepper and drizzle with olive oil.
15. Bake for 25-30 minutes until golden brown and cooked through. Cover the focaccia with aluminum foil in the last 10 minutes of baking to prevent the top from burning.
16. Cut into squares and serve.

NUTRITIONAL INFO (PER SERVING):

Calories: 250, Carbohydrates: 35 g, Cholesterol: 15 mg, Sodium: 380 mg, Protein: 6 g, Fats: 9 g, Sugar: 2 g, Fiber: 2 g

Vegetables & Sides

Desserts

PLUM CAKE

This recipe is very versatile. By changing the fruit or adding spices, nuts, or extracts, you can create a variety of flavors depending on the season and preferences. For example, adding almond extract blends beautifully with the natural flavor of the plums. If you purchased sweet plums, reduce the amount of sugar.

Crumb topping creates a delightful contrast of the textures of soft cake and juicy plums. The combination of flour, sugar, cinnamon, and butter creates a streusel-like filling that becomes golden and crispy after baking.

Some of the flour can be substituted with whole-grain alternatives.

VARIATIONS:

Vegans can use vegan butter and egg substitute for the pie dough and vegan butter for the crumb topping. Replace the fruit with berries, such as blueberries or raspberries.

12 servings   20 minutes   40 minutes

CAKE BATTER:

- 1 cup (240 g) unsalted butter, softened
- 1 cup (240 g) granulated sugar
- 3 large eggs
- 1 teaspoon vanilla extract
- 2 cups (260 g) all-purpose flour/ gluten-free flour
- 2 tsp. baking powder
- ½ tsp. salt

- ½ cup (120 ml) milk
- 12-15 ripe plums/peaches/ nectarines/ apricots, halved and pitted

CRUMB TOPPING:

- ½ cup (120 g) granulated sugar
- ½ cup (60 g) all-purpose flour
- ½ tsp. ground cinnamon
- ¼ cup (60 g) unsalted butter, chilled and cubed

HOW TO COOK:

1. Preheat the oven to 350°F (180°C). Line a sheet pan (13x9 inches/33x23 cm) with parchment paper.
2. Beat the softened butter and sugar until slightly fluffy.
3. Add vanilla extract and all eggs, beating after each egg.
4. Mix the dry ingredients (flour, salt, and baking powder) in a separate bowl.
5. Gradually add milk and the dry ingredients to the beaten butter and egg mixture. Mix until you have a homogeneous mixture.
6. Spread the batter evenly over the prepared sheet pan.
7. Arrange the halved plums cut side up on top of the batter, pressing them lightly into the batter.
8. Combine the sugar, flour, and ground cinnamon in a small bowl. Beat in the cooled butter until the mixture resembles coarse crumbs.
9. Sprinkle the crumble mixture evenly over the plums and dough.
10. Bake for 35-40 minutes until golden brown. Check with a toothpick inserted in the center of the pie.
11. Once cooled, cut into squares and serve.

NUTRITIONAL INFO (PER SERVING):

Calories: 320, Carbohydrates: 42 g, Cholesterol: 75 mg, Sodium: 180 mg, Protein: 4 g, Fats: 16 g, Sugar: 24 g, Fiber: 2 g

BROWNIES

It's crucial not to overbake the brownies. A slightly underbaked center is what you're aiming for, as it ensures a moist and puffy texture. They continue cooking while cooling.

Use a plastic knife or a knife soaked in hot water to cut the brownies into clean slices without tearing them.

VARIATIONS:

Substitute heavy cream for coconut cream. Use dairy-free chocolate chips.

For an extra spreadable texture, add an additional melted chocolate (½ cup/120 ml) to the batter.

***Peanut Butter Swirl:** Place peanut butter pieces on the brownie batter and swipe with a knife before baking.*

24 servings   15 minutes   30 minutes

INGREDIENTS:

BROWNIES:

- 1 cup (240 g) unsalted butter, melted
- 2 cups (400 g) granulated sugar
- 1 cup (200 g) light brown sugar
- 4 large eggs, at room temperature
- 2 teaspoons vanilla extract
- 1 cup (130 g) all-purpose flour/ gluten-free flour
- 1 cup (85 g) unsweetened cocoa powder

- 1 teaspoon salt
- 1 cup (175 g) semi-sweet chocolate chips
- 1 cup (125 g) nuts, chopped

TOPPING:

- 1 cup (175 g) semi-sweet chocolate chips
- ½ cup (120 ml) heavy cream
- Chopped nuts, for garnish (optional)

HOW TO COOK:

1. Preheat the oven to 350°F (180°C). Cover a sheet pan (13x18 inches/33x46 cm) with parchment paper.
2. Beat the softened butter and white and brown sugar until slightly fluffy.
3. Add vanilla extract and all eggs, beating after each egg.
4. Mix the dry ingredients (flour, cocoa powder, and salt) in a separate bowl. Combine the mixed dry ingredients and the wet ingredients.
5. Add chocolate chips and chopped nuts.
6. Spread the brownie batter evenly on the prepared sheet pan.
7. Bake for 25-30 minutes until a toothpick inserted in the center comes out with a small amount of moist crumbs.
8. Remove from oven and let cool completely.
9. Meanwhile, heat the heavy cream until it begins to boil. Remove from heat and add chocolate shavings. Leave for 2 minutes, then stir until smooth and shiny.
10. Spread the warm ganache over the cooled brownies. Sprinkle with nuts.
11. When the topping has been set, cut brownies into squares and serve.

NUTRITIONAL INFO (PER SERVING):

Calories: 300, Carbohydrates: 41 g, Cholesterol: 60 mg, Sodium: 120 mg, Protein: 4 g, Fats: 15 g, Sugar: 30 g, Fiber: 2 g

Desserts

STRAWBERRY PAVLOVA

Make sure the egg whites are room temperature and yolk-free to maximize volume. Whip the egg whites until they form stiff peaks, and ensure the sugar is completely dissolved to avoid a gritty texture.

Pavlova should cool completely in the oven, then it will not crack. Pavlova is best served fresh. If you prepare the pavlova in advance, spread toppings just before serving to preserve the crispness of the meringue.

VARIATIONS:

You can use different fruits like kiwi, blueberries, raspberries, or passion fruit for a colorful and flavorful filling.

For a twist, enrich the meringue mixture with cocoa powder to create a delectable chocolate-flavored pavlova. Complement the whipped cream with a sprinkle of chopped nuts (almonds or pistachios) for a delightful crunch.

12 servings   1 hour 15 minutes   1 hour

INGREDIENTS:

PAVLOVA:
- 6 large egg whites
- 1½ cups (300g) granulated sugar
- 1 tsp. vanilla extract
- 1 tsp. white vinegar
- 1 Tbsp. cornstarch/cornflour

TOPPING:
- 2 Tbsp. granulated sugar

- 2 cups (480ml) heavy cream/double cream
- 1 tsp. vanilla extract
- 2 cups (300g) fresh strawberries, hulled and quartered
- Zest of 1 lime
- Powdered sugar/icing sugar, for dusting

HOW TO COOK:

1. Preheat the oven to 275°F (135°C). Line a sheet pan (13x18 inches or 33x46 cm) with parchment paper.
2. Beat egg whites (no sugar yet) on medium speed until soft peaks form.
3. Add white sugar 1 tablespoon at a time while continuing to beat at high speed. Stiff peaks should form, and the mixture should become glossy. This will take about 8 to 10 minutes.
4. Gently add the vanilla extract, white vinegar, and cornstarch until you have a smooth mixture.
5. Spread the meringue mixture evenly over the prepared sheet pan, making it rectangular, about 1 inch (2.5 cm) thick.
6. Bake for 75 minutes until the pavlova is dry to the touch and lightly golden.
7. Turn off the oven and leave the pavlova in it with the door ajar for about 1 hour.
8. Whisk the heavy cream, granulated sugar, and vanilla extract until soft peaks form.
9. Spoon the whipped cream over the cooled meringue.
10. Arrange the strawberries cut into quarters in an even layer on top of the whipped cream.
11. Sprinkle the strawberries with lime zest and sprinkle with powdered sugar.
12. Cut the pavlova into squares and serve immediately.

NUTRITIONAL INFO (PER SERVING):

Calories: 220, Carbohydrates: 33 g, Cholesterol: 50 mg, Sodium: 35 mg, Protein: 3 g, Fats: 9 g, Sugar: 29 g, Fiber: 1 g

Desserts

PEARS WITH BLUE CHEESE

I love pears for their sweetness, juiciness, and versatility. They can be used in savory dishes as well as in sweet dishes. Their natural sweetness pairs well with strong cheeses, such as blue cheese, with its bold and tangy flavor. Fresh thyme adds a flavorful and earthy note to the dish.

This recipe is a great example of how simple ingredients can be turned into an elegant and sophisticated dessert. The presentation of baked pears makes it perfect for dinner parties and special occasions. Despite the gourmet look, this recipe is quick and easy to prepare. With minimal ingredients and simple steps, it's a great last-minute dessert option.

VARIATIONS:

Replace blue cheese with goat cheese for a milder flavor. Maple syrup instead of honey will give a different sweetness. Add cinnamon or nutmeg for a warm, spicy flavor.

6 servings   15 minutes   20 minutes

INGREDIENTS:

- 3 large pears (Bosc or Anjou), halved and cored
- 2 Tbsp. (30 ml) honey
- ½ cup (60 g) blue cheese, crumbled
- ½ cup (60 g) walnuts/pecans, chopped

- 1 Tbsp. fresh thyme leaves
- Pinch of sea salt
- Freshly ground black pepper to taste

HOW TO COOK:

1. Preheat the oven to 375°F (190°C). Line a sheet pan with parchment paper.
2. Cut the pears in half and remove the core. Arrange the pear halves cut side up on the prepared baking tray.
3. Pour honey evenly over the pear halves.
4. Sprinkle the pears with crumbled blue cheese and chopped walnuts.
5. Sprinkle fresh thyme leaves on top and season with sea salt and ground black pepper.
6. Bake for 20-25 minutes until the pears are tender and the blue cheese is melted and lightly golden.
7. Serve the baked pears warm with Greek yogurt or vanilla ice cream, drizzled with a little honey if desired.

NUTRITIONAL INFO (PER SERVING):

Calories: 170, Carbohydrates: 22 g, Cholesterol: 8 mg, Sodium: 100 mg, Protein: 4 g, Fats: 8 g, Sugar: 16 g, Fiber: 3 g

CHOCOLATE CHIP BLONDIES

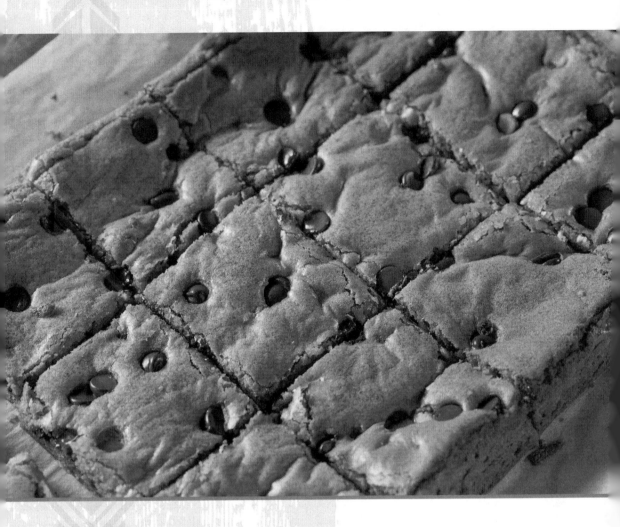

We have one unspoken rule in our family for baking desserts using a sheet pan – we bake fruit and berry pastry in the summer and cookies, blondies, and brownies in the winter. Blondies with chocolate drops or any other additions are just such an autumn/winter recipe for cozy, cold cocoa evenings. I'd be lying if I said it was only loved by our kids. My wife and I and our friends enjoy indulging in these delicious bars not only on weekends but also on weekdays, thanks to the simple and quick cooking.

VARIATIONS:

Add 1 cup (120 g) of chopped nuts (walnuts/pecans/almonds) to the batter to give it a crunch. For a different flavor, replace half of the chocolate shavings with white chocolate shavings. Add ½ cup (75 g) dried cranberries or sultanas for a fruity touch.

24 squares 15 minutes 25 minutes

INGREDIENTS:

- 1 cup (225 g) butter, melted
- 2 cups (400 g) light brown sugar
- ½ cup (100 g) granulated sugar
- 3 large eggs
- 2 tsp. vanilla extract

- 2½ cups (315 g) all-purpose flour
- 1 tsp. cinnamon/½ tsp. nutmeg
- 1 tsp. baking powder
- ½ tsp. salt
- 1½ cups (260 g) chocolate chips

HOW TO COOK:

1. Preheat the oven to 350°F (175°C). Grease a 13x18 inch (33x46 cm) sheet pan or line it with parchment paper.
2. Combine the melted butter, light brown sugar, and granulated sugar. Mix well until smooth. Beat in the eggs one at a time, then add the vanilla extract.
3. In a separate bowl, whisk the plain flour, baking powder, spices, and salt. Add the dry ingredients to the whipped mixture 2-3 spoonfuls at a time, stirring until fully combined.
4. Gently add the chocolate chips, making sure they are evenly distributed throughout the dough.
5. Spread the batter evenly over the prepared sheet pan, leveling it with a spatula.
6. Bake for 20-25 minutes until the edges of the blondies are golden brown. Check with a toothpick inserted in the center.
7. Cool in the sheet pan. Once completely cooled, cut into 24 squares.
8. These brownies are delicious on their own, but for a more satisfying treat, serve them with vanilla ice cream or caramel sauce.

NUTRITIONAL INFO (PER SERVING):

Calories: 285, Carbohydrates: 39 g, Cholesterol: 45 mg, Sodium: 100 mg, Protein: 3 g, Fats: 13 g, Sugar: 27 g, Fiber: 1 g

ABOUT ME

My name is Christopher Lester, and I've always been drawn to the culinary arts. From an early age, **I liked the magic that happens in the kitchen**, where simple ingredients are transformed into extraordinary dishes. Over the years, I have honed my skills and acquired unique techniques, becoming a renowned culinary wizard and flavor magician.

My journey began with a thirst for knowledge and a desire to learn from the best. I sought out the biggest names in the culinary realm to soak up their wisdom. From celebrity chefs to seasoned culinary experts, I was like a sponge, soaking up their expertise and incorporating it into my repertoire.

But my world didn't just revolve around the kitchen. I had two beautiful daughters who brought joy and laughter into my life. When I wasn't enchanting the culinary world with my creations, I was spending time with them and my faithful companion in the kitchen, Jack, our beloved family dog. Together, we would go on adventures, explore the wonders of nature, and share precious moments.

In my free time, I loved to put on my worn apron, a symbol of my culinary prowess, and invite friends and family to gather around the table. The joy of creating festive dishes for my loved ones was incomparable. **Tantalizing aromas filled the air, heralding the beginning of the culinary feast.**

WHAT TO READ NEXT

Dutch Oven Cookbook

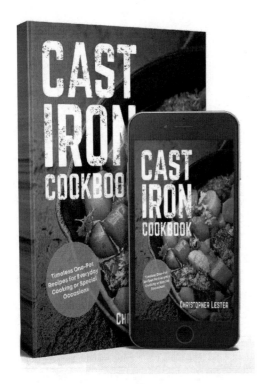

Cast Iron Cookbook

Made in the USA
Monee, IL
11 December 2024

73170257R00061